The Bible Speaks Today

Series editors: J. A. Motyer (OT)
John Stott (NT)
Derek Tidball (Bible Themes)

The Message of Proverbs

Wisdom for life

The Bible Speaks Today: Old Testament series

The Message of Genesis 1 – 11
The dawn of creation
David Atkinson

The Message of Genesis 12 – 50
From Abraham to Joseph
Joyce G. Baldwin

The Message of Exodus
The days of our pilgrimage
Alec Motyer

The Message of Leviticus
Free to be holy
Derek Tidball

The Message of Numbers
Journey to the promised land
Raymond Brown

The Message of Deuteronomy
Not by bread alone
Raymond Brown

The Message of Judges
Grace abounding
Michael Wilcock

The Message of Ruth
The wings of refuge
David Atkinson

The Message of Samuel
*Personalities, potential, politics
and power*
Mary Evans

The Message of Chronicles
One church, one faith, one Lord
Michael Wilcock

The Message of Nehemiah
God's servant in a time of change
Raymond Brown

The Message of Job
Suffering and grace
David Atkinson

The Message of Psalms 1 – 72
Songs for the people of God
Michael Wilcock

The Message of Psalms 73 – 150
Songs for the people of God
Michael Wilcock

The Message of Proverbs
Wisdom for life
David Atkinson

The Message of Ecclesiastes
*A time to mourn, and a time to
dance*
Derek Kidner

The Message of the Song of Songs
The lyrics of love
Tom Gledhill

The Message of Isaiah
On eagles' wings
Barry Webb

The Message of Jeremiah
Against wind and tide
Derek Kidner

The Message of Ezekiel
A new heart and a new spirit
Christopher J. H. Wright

The Message of Daniel
The Lord is King
Ronald S. Wallace

The Message of Hosea
Love to the loveless
Derek Kidner

**The Message of Joel, Micah and
Habakkuk**
Listening to the voice of God
David Prior

The Message of Amos
The day of the lion
Alec Motyer

The Message of Jonah
Presence in the storm
Rosemary Nixon

The Message of Zechariah
Your kingdom come
Barry Webb

The Message of Proverbs

Wisdom for life

David Atkinson

*Archdeacon of Lewisham,
Diocese of Southwark, London*

Inter-Varsity Press

Inter-Varsity Press
38 De Montfort Street, Leicester LE1 7GP, England
Email: ivp@ivp-editorial.co.uk
Website: www.ivpbooks.com

First published 1996
Reprinted 1999, 2000, 2002, 2003, 2005

British Library Cataloguing in Publication Data
A catalogue record for this book is available from the British Library.

ISBN–10: 0-85111-166-1
ISBN–13: 978-0-85111-166-7

Set in 10/11pt Stempel Garamond
Typeset in Great Britain by Parker Typesetting Service, Leicester
Printed and bound in Great Britain by Creative Print & Design (Wales) Ltd, Ebbw Vale.

Inter-Varsity Press is the publishing division of the Universities and Colleges Christian Fellowship (formerly the Inter-Varsity Fellowship), a student movement linking Christian Unions in universities and colleges throughout Great Britain, and a member movement of the International Fellowship of Evangelical Students. For information about local and national activities write to UCCF, 38 De Montfort Street, Leicester, LE1 7GP, email us at email@uccf.org.uk, or visit the UCCF website at www.uccf.org.uk.

Contents

| BST | The Bible Speaks Today

GENERAL PREFACE

THE BIBLE SPEAKS TODAY describes three series of expositions, based on the books of the Old and New Testaments, and on Bible themes that run through the whole of Scripture. Each series is characterized by a threefold ideal:

- to expound the biblical text with accuracy
- to relate it to contemporary life, and
- to be readable.

These books are, therefore, not 'commentaries', for the commentary seeks rather to elucidate the text than to apply it, and tends to be a work rather of reference than of literature. Nor, on the other hand, do they contain the kinds of 'sermons' that attempt to be contemporary and readable without taking Scripture seriously enough. The contributors to *The Bible Speaks Today* series are all united in their convictions that God still speaks through what he has spoken, and that nothing is more necessary for the life, health and growth of Christians than that they should hear what the Spirit is saying to them through his ancient – yet ever modern – Word.

ALEC MOTYER
JOHN STOTT
DEREK TIDBALL
Series editors

To the theological faculties at Hope College
and at Western Theological Seminary, Holland,
Michigan, from a grateful visitor

Author's preface

An early version of this book was being thought about one February as I sat on the fifth floor of the magnificent theological library at Western Seminary, looking out over the dazzling Michigan snow. Part of it was drafted beside Long Pond in New England one glorious summer. Most of it was written in our house at the Elephant and Castle in London, not many hundred metres from where people live in cardboard boxes under Waterloo Bridge, and where seventeen-year-old Stephen is probably at this moment asking passers-by in the underpass if they have any change to spare. The contrast was salutary. The book of Proverbs itself moves between the glory and delight of God's creation and the powerlessness of poverty.

When I first accepted the invitation to write this exposition I did not realize quite what I was taking on. The more I have explored this part of the wisdom literature of the Hebrew Bible, the more I have been both impressed by the continuing topicality of its teaching, and frustrated by trying to bring its apparently disorganized mass of material into some sort of accessible form.

On the one hand, despite the centuries which separate us from the authors of these sayings, the unchanging continuities of human existence remain: making friends, coping with sexuality, handling money, responding to poverty, making a living, learning through loss, muddling through difficulties, facing death, and so on. These are constant human themes, and Proverbs addresses them all. Wisdom is about helping people to cope; about seeing things in a fresh way which gives new resources for living; and about working out what living for God means in the ordinarinesses of daily life. The book of Proverbs brings many of these themes to life in vivid, imaginative, often humorous pictures. It puts a mirror up to our behaviour and says, 'Are you like this? Is there a better way to live?'

On the other hand, the greater part of the book of Proverbs seems to have no shape or pattern to it, and is simply a series of collections of clever sayings. Part of my difficulty and frustration in writing this book was in deciding how to try to expound such a varied tapestry of ideas in a way which might both be helpful in the modern world and also be faithful to the text as it stands. One approach which I found extremely helpful was the one which suggests that to see many of these sayings as shaped by a fourfold structure helps us tease out the basic moral and spiritual values which the writers of Proverbs assume. Thus many of the proverbs seem to be structured in a way which suggests that 'this' is better than 'that'. I found it very illuminating to work through the whole book asking myself of each proverb, 'What is the most important moral and spiritual value being assumed or upheld by the writer here?' I made a list of these, and this forms the basis for my discussion of what I have called 'Wisdom's values'.

It may be helpful to outline my approach to the whole book. The first nine chapters of Proverbs are rather different from what follows. In them the figure of Wisdom – a woman who embodies the wisdom of God – is portrayed in word pictures. My introductory section, 'The Wisdom of God', tries to fill in the contours of this portrait. Part 1 then looks at some of the teaching material of these first nine chapters – the sorts of questions the wisdom teachers were wanting their pupils to learn, and how they went about teaching them. Then in Part 3 I open up the question of the literary structure of Proverbs, and the fourfold pattern to which I referred; I also look at Wisdom's imagination and the wonderful artistry which this book displays. Finally I cover the rest of Proverbs under the heading of Wisdom's Values', trying to make links between the moral precepts of ancient Israel, and the relevance of such teaching for Christian people today. My confidence in making this attempt is the conviction that the character of God which is displayed in the figure of Wisdom in the book of Proverbs is the character which we see embodied in Jesus Christ. He is God's Wisdom, and to know him is to know the ways and will of God for how to behave in his world.

One of the great delights of the past few years for me was the opportunity to spend two terms teaching as Northrup Visiting Professor at Hope College, Holland, Michigan. Not only did they allow us a much appreciated family trip to Disneyland as part of the deal, but one of the friends I made in Holland was Professor Robert Coughenour of Western Theological Seminary. His own deep researches into the wisdom literature have been a source of inspiration to me and I wish to acknowledge my debt to him, his published writing, and his kindness in also sending me some of his unpublished work. As a mark of gratitude to him, and to other friends from Hope College, I am pleased to dedicate this book to the theological faculties there.

As with the other contributions I have made to this series, I have been enormously helped by the constructive criticism, helpful suggestions and spiritual wisdom offered to me by Alec Motyer, and by the support of Colin Duriez at IVP. I am most grateful to them both.

DAVID ATKINSON
Southwark Cathedral

Bibliography

Anderson, B. W., *The Living World of the Old Testament* (Longmans, 2nd edition 1967).

Anderson, G. W., *A Critical Introduction to the Old Testament* (Duckworth, 1959).

Clements, R. E., *Wisdom in Theology* (Paternoster, 1992).

Coughenour, R. A., 'The Wisdom Literature of the Bible', and other unpublished documents, kindly made available to me by the author.

Goldingay, J., 'Proverbs' in the *New Bible Commentary* (IVP, 1995 edition).

Groome, T. H., *Christian Religious Education* (Harper and Row, 1981).

Henry, Matthew, *Exposition of the Old and New Testaments* (1708–10, various editions).

Horton, R. F., *The Book of Proverbs*, The Expositor's Bible (Hodder and Stoughton, 1911).

Hubbard, D. A., *Proverbs*, The Communicator's Commentary (Word, 1989).

Kidner, Derek, *Proverbs*, Tyndale Old Testament Commentaries (IVP, 1964).

————*The Wisdom of Proverbs, Job and Ecclesiastes* (IVP, 1985).

McKane, W., *Proverbs: A New Approach*, Old Testament Library (SCM, 1975).

Perry, T. A., *Wisdom Literature and the Structure of Proverbs* (Pennsylvania State University Press, 1993).

Scott, R. B. Y., *Proverbs; Ecclesiastes*, Anchor Bible (Doubleday, 1965).

Toy, C. H., *The Book of Proverbs*, International Critical Commentary (T. and T. Clark, 1899).

Whybray, R. N., *Wisdom in Proverbs*, Studies in Biblical Theology 45 (SCM, 1965).

————*Proverbs*, New Century Bible Commentary (Marshall Pickering, 1994).

The wisdom of God

How can God be known? There is, of course, a sense in which God cannot be known. God is beyond our knowing. The Orthodox tradition, which many in the West are discovering or rediscovering, reminds us of the foolishness of trying to comprehend and understand God. God is mystery, and the language of the negative (God is invisible, intangible, and so on) reminds us that it is often easier to say what or who God is not, than to say who or what God is. Certainly, a god whom we claim to know through our own reasoning is not the God of the Bible or of the Christian church. Such a god is more likely to be an idol made in our own image. And yet there is another, and vital, sense in which God can be known. God is known as God makes himself known. There is a parallel here with our knowledge of human persons. There are people of whom we say, 'I do not know him'; 'She is very hard to know.' Even in human relationships, there is much we can know about a person, without knowing the person. We know Julia as far as Julia makes herself known. So it is with our knowledge of God. We can know God in so far as God is willing to make himself known. We can know, not the fullness of God, but 'the things revealed' (Dt. 29:29). As St Paul says of himself in his letter to Corinth, so we can say of God: he is 'unknown, and yet well known' (2 Cor. 6:9, RSV).

But how does God make himself known? The answer of Christian faith is that this is accomplished supremely and personally in Jesus Christ. Jesus Christ is the one human person in whom God's mind and spirit are perfectly expressed. Jesus is truly 'the image of the invisible God' (Col. 1:15). He is the one by whom we measure every other way in which God is revealed.

Of course there are many other ways in which something of God can be known in this world, ways which we evaluate by their congruence with God's self-disclosure in Jesus.

For many people, God is known in experience. God is felt to be near to us, his presence filling all things. It can often be at the times when we experience deep emotions of love or grief that we sense the presence of God near us or within us. There are experiences which Peter Berger, in his book *A Rumour of Angels*,[1] calls 'signals of transcendence'. Some psychologists, of whom perhaps Abraham Maslow is best known, refer to 'peak experiences', which religious people often interpret as experiences of God.[2] Some of these fit into the categories William James referred to in his famous Gifford Lectures at the turn of the century: 'the feelings, acts and experiences of individual men in their solitude, so far as they apprehend themselves to stand in relation to whatever they may consider the divine'.[3] The researches of the late Professor Sir Alister Hardy at what was initially called the 'Religious Experience Research Unit' in Oxford (now the Alister Hardy Centre) have shown the surprising frequency with which people admit to being aware of 'a presence or power different from their everyday self'.[4] Clearly, many Christian people would want to say much more about their experiences of God than this, and would often want to set them much more firmly than either James or Hardy does in the corporate context of Christian fellowship. But this research is sufficient to remind us that in the ordinary business of living in God's world, there are sometimes extraordinary experiences which function for more people than we usually imagine as 'signals of transcendence'.

Then there are experiences of wonder, and the excitement of being alive in a wonderful world, of which Michael Mayne, Dean of Westminster, writes in his letters to his godchildren, *This Sunrise of Wonder*.[5] This beautiful book uncovers the author's delight in the natural world, in literature, music and art, opening up, for those whose eyes are not closed, vistas of beauty and joy which find their meaning in God.

There can, for example, be a sense of God's majesty when we are caught up in the wonder of the created order. To stand on the high road overlooking the great gorges and waterfalls in the Yosemite National Park, to fly over the Grand Canyon, to stand and look up at a snow-covered mountain peak, to watch the sun going down over a Scottish loch, to be alone in the dark under a clear starry sky – these can give us glimpses of glory.

The wonderful order of the created world can show us something of God.

---

[1] Penguin, 1970.

[2] *E.g.* A. Maslow, *Toward a Psychology of Being* (Van Nostrand, 1968); *cf.* also idem, *The Farther Reaches of Human Nature* (Viking, 1971), *passim.*

[3] W. James, *The Varieties of Religious Experience*, Lecture II (Longmans, 1902).

[4] A. Hardy, *The Spiritual Nature of Man* (Oxford, 1979); *cf.* also David Hay, *Religious Experience Today* (Mowbray, 1990).

[5] Fount, 1995.

As Thomas Traherne wrote in the seventeenth century:

It is a natural effect of infinite Wisdome to make every of its Treasures suitable to its own excellence. And that the Wisdome of God has done, by making the smallest Thing in his Kingdome infinitely Serviceable in its Place, and Station, for the manifesting of his Wisdome, Goodness and Glory to the Eye of a clear Beholder. And this he has done by making all his Kingdome one intire Object, and everything in it a Part of that Whole. Relating to all the innumerable Parts, receiving a Beauty from all, and communicating a Beauty to all, even to all objects throughout all Eternity.[6]

The same thought is picked up by Gerard Manley Hopkins:

The world is charged with the grandeur of God.
It will flame out like shining from shook foil;
It gathers to a greatness, like the ooze of oil
Crushed. Why do men then now not reck his rod?
Generations have trod, have trod, have trod;
And all is seared with trade; bleared, smeared with toil;
And wears man's smudge and shares man's smell: the soil
Is bare now, nor can foot feel, being shod.

And for all this, nature is never spent;
There lives the dearest freshness deep down things;
And though the last lights off the black West went
Oh, morning, at the brown brink eastward, springs –
Because the Holy Ghost over the bent
World broods with warm breast and with ah! bright wings.[7]

Hopkins coined the word 'inscape' for that collection of data presented to our senses which together make up the rich 'oneness' of things in the natural world. About 'God's Grandeur' he writes: 'I thought how sadly beauty of inscape was unknown and buried away from simple people and yet how near at hand it was if they had eyes to see it and it could be called out everywhere again.'[8]

God's presence may also be experienced in the moral values which confront us in the form of obligations and duties. The psalmist couples knowledge of God in the wonderful order of creation with knowledge of God through the moral law: 'The heavens declare the

---

[6] Thomas Traherne, *Christian Ethicks*, quoted in G. Dowell, *Enjoying the World: The Rediscovery of Thomas Traherne* (Mowbray, 1990), p. 55.

[7] 'God's Grandeur'.

[8] Quoted in W. H. Gardner's Introduction to the Penguin Classics edition of Gerard Manley Hopkins, *Poems and Prose*, p. xxi.

glory of God . . . The law of the LORD is perfect, reviving the soul' (Ps. 19:1, 7). We know, deep inside us, what moral obligation means, and that it confronts us from without. Moral obligation is not simply something we make up for ourselves. We know that recoiling in horror against genocide in Rwanda or 'ethnic cleansing' in Bosnia is not a matter of personal taste and preference for those who do not like that sort of thing. There is an objective moral order which confronts us. As Christians, we understand this in relation to the will of God.

For some while in recent decades there have been moral philosophers who have argued that morality, if it means anything at all, is essentially something private and personal. That usually means subjective and relative. More recently, however, there has been a recovery of the fact that moral obligation has an objective dimension (which ordinary common sense tells most of us anyhow). For example, Charles Taylor argues that 'Even the sense that the significance of my life comes from its being chosen . . . depends on the understanding that independent of my will there is something noble, courageous, and hence significant in giving shape to my own life'.[9] From a rather different starting-point, Iris Murdoch speaks of the concept of good as being 'forced upon us'. 'The sovereign Good is not an empty receptacle into which the arbitrary will places objects of its choice. It is something which we all experience as a creative force.'[10] Christian believers identify that source of moral value with God.

God may also, and perhaps even more fully, be found in the personal communion of love we may have with another person. This love is freeing and creative, and points beyond itself to a meaning and a significance which are in some sense 'given'. This, too, reaches beyond personal subjective choice. There is something which addresses me from beyond. The Anglican forms of the marriage service use the language of gift: 'Marriage is given that . . .' There can be a significance to our loving and our creativity, often found in art or music, in ecstatic joy or in the deepest sorrow, which is, as it were, given to us, drawing us into itself, and bringing into view horizons beyond ourselves in which meaning is found.

There is another way in which God can be known, and that is in the stillness. It is fascinating how many of the psalms speak of 'waiting' for God.[11] Some of these psalms come, of course, out of situations of personal struggle, national uncertainty, imminence of battle, or a sense of individual or social sinfulness. In Psalm 62:1, for

[9] C. Taylor, *The Ethics of Authenticity* (Harvard University Press, 1991), p. 39.
[10] I. Murdoch, *Metaphysics as a Guide to Morals* (Penguin, 1992), p. 507.
[11] *E.g.* Pss. 33:20; 37:34; 40:1; 130.

example, the poet, recognizing that much in his situation is uncertain, comments: 'My soul finds rest in God alone.' Waiting for God became a source of inner energy. As Psalm 46:10 puts it, 'Be still, and know . . .' Or, as T. S. Eliot might have put it, 'Be still and dance.' 'At the still point of the turning world', he says, is where the dance is, and without that point 'there would be no dance'.[12] Does this mean that in the still moment, in the centred moment, in the fully lived present moment, there is a coming together of stillness and movement? 'It is the pivotal point of stillness', says Harry Blamires, 'that makes movement possible, the centre around which the dance is ordered, and without which therefore meaningful life would be impossible.'[13] It is from and around the still point that the dance of joy-filled, meaningful living is possible, and finds its energy.

In a myriad ways, therefore, in nature and love, music and art, beauty and fear, activity and stillness, God's presence and his nature can be discerned, appreciated, felt. But the test by which we measure these experiences and understandings, and by which we distinguish them from an authoritarian conscience, or a social consensus, or some drug-induced religious-like experience of agony or ecstasy, is their congruence with the way God has made himself personally known in Jesus Christ.

The God whom Jesus Christ reveals is the Creator whose ordering wisdom lies behind everything that exists, whose moral character gives meaning to our awareness of right and wrong, and whose Holy Spirit infuses us with life, light, love and creativity. The wisdom, the values and the Spirit of God are seen in Jesus. As St Paul puts it in his first letter to the Corinthians: '[God] is the source of your life in Christ Jesus, whom God made our wisdom, our righteousness and sanctification and redemption' (1 Cor. 1:30, RSV), which must at least mean that Jesus Christ, as God's gift, became for us the means by which we know God's wisdom, righteousness and spiritual life.

Such terms come readily to St Paul's mind, because they are deeply rooted in the traditions of the covenant people of God. The book of Proverbs is one example of what is often called the Hebrew wisdom literature, in which many of the themes we have been discussing are present. Other examples in the Bible are the books of Job and Ecclesiastes. In the Apocrypha also we find, for example, the books of *Ecclesiasticus* and *Wisdom*. Much of this may have been in St Paul's mind as he related the themes of the wisdom literature to Jesus. In fact, as we shall see in much more detail in due course, it is fascinating how the language which St Paul uses of Christ in Colossians 1:15–18 is very close to the picture of Wisdom in

---

[12] T. S. Eliot, *Four Quartets*: 'Burnt Norton'.
[13] Harry Blamires, *Words Unheard* (Methuen, 1969), p. 21.

19

Proverbs 8:22ff., and both relate back to the poem in Genesis 1:1: 'In the beginning God created the heavens and the earth.' The Wisdom of God in the Old Testament, and the Christ of the New, are both at the heart of God's creativity and purpose for his world. There are similar resonances in Hebrews 1:1–3. The writer's portrait there of the Son of God, the heir of all things, through whom God created the world, who reflects God's glory and upholds the universe by his word of power, is very close to the portrait of Wisdom in Proverbs 8. In much the same way, the prologue of John's gospel (Jn. 1:1–5) mirrors something of the picture of Wisdom which is painted in Proverbs, when it speaks of the Word who was in the beginning with God, through whom all things were made – a Word that gives life and light.

The book of Proverbs also features in a number of other places in the New Testament. When the writer to the Hebrews, for example, is explaining that some aspects of Christian suffering may be understood as discipline from God to help us grow in holiness, he draws on Proverbs 3 (Heb. 12:5–6 and Pr. 3:11–12). The letters of both James (Jas. 4:6) and Peter (1 Pet. 5:5) quote Proverbs 3:34 when they assert that 'God opposes the proud, but gives grace to the humble'. Earlier in the first letter of Peter (1 Pet. 4:18), there is a quotation from Proverbs 11:31. Romans 12:20 draws on Proverbs 25:21; 2 Peter 2:22 quotes from Proverbs 26:11.

There is ancient wisdom to draw on for the New Testament writers as they try to find words in which to describe God's self-disclosure in Jesus Christ. It is ancient wisdom on which we, too, can draw, as we try to understand Jesus the Christ and learn to follow him as disciples. We can learn from Paul, Peter, and the writer to the Hebrews. But we also come to a reading of the book of Proverbs from the perspective of the New Testament texts, and from a long history of the church's thinking about the revelation of God made known to us in Jesus. As Jesus himself says, in him there is 'something greater' than the wisdom of Solomon (Mt. 12:41–42, RSV). Our faith in Christ now puts these Old Testament texts into a different focus. We approach them not as the earliest readers did, but as Christian people, reading the texts back through our own experiences of Christ and that of generations of Christian people.

It is not only that our understanding of Jesus Christ is illuminated by themes found in the wisdom literature; it is also that every path to true wisdom – every route by which we come truly to know God – leads us by way of Jesus Christ. In him all our knowledge of God, through experience, wonder, morality, reverence, love and so on, is brought into focus. These are some of the themes from which the book of Proverbs draws.

So we need a conversation between the ancient book of Proverbs and our Christian understanding of Jesus Christ. Through this we may find that the Old Testament themes illuminate what we want to say about Jesus, but also that, looking back on the Old Testament from the vantage-point of our Christian faith, what we know about Jesus may illuminate the message of Proverbs.

Where are the proverbs from?

The proverbs of Solomon son of David, king of Israel . . . (1:1).

The opening verse of the book of Proverbs indicates that there is a close link between the tradition of proverbial wisdom and King Solomon, the son of great King David, who ruled Israel from about 961 to 922 BC, and whose story is told in the first book of Kings. He was certainly known for his wisdom, as we read in 1 Kings 4:29–34:

> God gave Solomon wisdom and understanding beyond measure, and largeness of mind like the sand on the seashore, so that Solomon's wisdom surpassed the wisdom of all the people of the east, and all the wisdom of Egypt. For he was wiser than all other men . . . He also uttered three thousand proverbs; and his songs were a thousand and five . . . men came from all peoples to hear the wisdom of Solomon (RSV).

There is good reason (and many Old Testament specialists are returning to this view) that where Proverbs ascribes material to Solomon, this may be taken at face value and not simply ascribed to his traditional patronage of wisdom. There are some sections of the book which are attributed to other authors: Agur and Lemuel are mentioned (30:1; 31:1), as well as an unnamed group of 'the wise' (22:17, which includes material worded very similarly to an Egyptian writing, *Instruction of Amenemope*; and 24:23). Hezekiah, a later king of Judah from 715 to 687 BC, is said to have got his men to copy out some of Solomon's proverbs, and these are recorded in Proverbs 25:1ff. So what we have now as 'the book of Proverbs' is a collection of collections, probably having passed through the hands of several editors and several editions, from several different sources and times, brought together as another resource, alongside the law, the prophecies and the histories in the Old Testament, by which the people of God could be helped to learn something of the ways and wisdom of God.

With the slow and easy trading across the Middle East, there was undoubtedly much mingling of ideas, and it is not surprising to find similarities between the wisdom teachings of different cultures. The Old Testament itself shows that wisdom was a feature of the culture of Israel's neighbours. (Egypt is referred to, for example, in Gn. 41:8; Ex. 7:11; 1 Ki. 4:30; Is. 19:11; Babylon in Is. 44:25; Je. 50:35; 51:57; and Edom in Je. 49:7; Ob. 8 and Jb. 2:11). Egyptian and Mesopotamian writers sought to explore the questions of life and death in the light of their own background faith. The book of Proverbs is exploring these same questions from its basis of faith in Yahweh, the covenant God of Israel. The proverbs are concerned with the practicalities of living in God's world, with 'life skills'; but they assume that all this is rooted in religious life and worship. Proverbs weaves together threads of moral and religious colours with others which are more concerned with getting on, doing well and being happy. We find experience, wonder, morality, love, and many other themes. The resulting tapestry is one in which all these aspects of living for God in God's world belong together. There is no split between what is 'sacred' and what is 'secular'. Life is to be lived to the full before God, and the proverbs give some pointers about how to manage and how to cope. Proverbs, says G. W. Anderson succinctly, 'illustrates several aspects of Hebrew wisdom literature; its intense concern with character and conduct, its interest in mundane affairs of daily life, its seemingly prudential ethics, its emphasis on the religious character of wisdom.'[14] Derek Kidner elaborates this last phrase. 'You have to be *godly* to be wise; and this is not because godliness pays, but because the only wisdom by which you can handle everyday things in conformity with their nature is the wisdom by which they were divinely made and ordered.' He links this especially to the exploration of the nature of wisdom which we find in Proverbs 8, and to which we must give our attention in due course: 'Proverbs 8, which states this superlatively, is therefore far from being a non-functional pinnacle of the book's eloquence, but is rather an exposure of the main framework of its thought.'[15]

Who are the proverbs for?

The people to whom we owe the wisdom literature in our Old Testament are called 'the wise' in Jeremiah 18:18, a distinctive group of those who spoke from God alongside the prophets and the priests. Were they in some cases the same people as the scribes or advisers to the king, referred to in 2 Samuel 8:17? Sometimes 'the wise' got into trouble with the prophets; sometimes the prophets had to warn people against those who were wise in their own eyes (*cf.* Is. 29:13–15). Whereas the prophets tended to focus on the global scene,

[14] G. W. Anderson, p. 189.
[15] Kidner, *Proverbs*, p. 32.

upholding God as the sovereign Lord of the nations, the wise men tended to concentrate on matters of individual and social ethics. So who were the wise men writing for?

It may very well be that some of this literature was developed in training-schools for the intellectual and social élite. Certainly Hebrew wisdom flourished at the royal court. Mention is made not only of Solomon, but of King Hezekiah and of Lemuel, who is also called a king. Chapters 16 and 31 of Proverbs have a good deal to say about royal protocol: how kings should behave, and how their courtiers are to show appropriate respect. This is not, of course, to limit the application of wisdom to the young in the royal court. Much of it is universal in scope. Some of the book reflects the life of rich, landowning people, able to afford luxuries (wisdom is compared to jewels, *e.g.* 3:15; and to good food and wine, *e.g.* 9:1–6). Sometimes the setting seems to be the city: Wisdom calls from noisy street corners (*e.g.* 1:20). At other times, the setting is more rural or agricultural. The poor man is not addressed in Proverbs: he is rather to be cared for by those to whom Proverbs is directed. Most of the teaching is also given to men, and women seem to feature only in relation to men (as wives or mothers or adulteresses). All this reinforces the view that some, at least, of Proverbs (especially from the first nine chapters) is primarily written as instruction for the young men of Israel who are being trained up for their place in the court. These are the future leaders. How important it is that they should be trained to understand the ways of God, and see the implications of their faith in Yahweh in all details of day-to-day life! It is on such as these that the future health of God's people depends. That primary focus may explain why the poor are more treated as victims than addressed as neighbours, and why women on the whole get a rather marginal deal in Proverbs.

This is not to say, we emphasize, that the wisdom enshrined in Proverbs is not applicable to other people. Rich and poor, male and female, courtier and servant, leader and artisan – all are human beings made in God's image, with the same basic concerns for food and shelter, sex and marriage, work and leisure, managing relation-ships, and anxieties about health and about death. Much of chapters 10 – 22 seems to reflect more ordinary, prudential wisdom about how to cope with life.[16] The relative importance of various needs will, of course, be different for different people. So, while part of the focus of some of the early chapters of Proverbs may be the young man at school, there is something here for everyone.

[16] *Cf. e.g.* E. W. Heaton, *The Hebrew Kingdoms* (Oxford University Press, 1968), p. 165: 'Wisdom is the ability to cope.'

What are the proverbs for?

So what are the proverbs for? The opening paragraph of chapter 1 gives us some insights.

The proverbs of Solomon son of David, king of Israel:

> *²for attaining wisdom and discipline;*
>   *for understanding words of insight;*
> *³for acquiring a disciplined and prudent life,*
>   *doing what is right and just and fair;*
> *⁴for giving prudence to the simple,*
>   *knowledge and discretion to the young –*
> *⁵let the wise listen and add to their learning,*
>   *and let the discerning get guidance –*
> *⁶for understanding proverbs and parables,*
>   *the sayings and riddles of the wise.*

These verses set out some of the purposes of the editor of this collection: to educate people in their knowledge and understanding; to give instruction in wise dealing, righteousness, justice and equity; especially to help the young discover discretion at a time of particular vulnerability for them; and to impart certain skills in the business of living.

Several words here form a cluster of similar meanings: *wisdom, discipline, understanding, insight, discretion, learning, guidance.* In the context of the book of Proverbs these are all to do with education, the discovery of the guiding principles of life, a 'practical wisdom' which helps people to find their way. Our word 'education' is actually not a bad definition of the word the NIV translates *discipline.* We find a New Testament counterpart in Hebrews 12:5, which discusses the way a good father brings up his children. The meanings of many of these words overlap; used together they strengthen and emphasize the teacher's meaning. *Wisdom* is the overarching term – a word which, as we explore further into the book of Proverbs, becomes the name of a woman whom we discover to be God's counterpart in the creative processes. We will refer to her with the capital letter: Wisdom. As Toy notes,[17] 'wisdom' is a word used to cover practical sagacity, the skill of the artisan, acquaintance with facts, learning, skill in expounding secret things, statesmanship, and knowledge of right living in the highest sense: moral and religious intelligence. When people respond to Wisdom, they are obedient, prudent and secure; they have understanding, and find that

[17] Toy, Introduction and p. 5.

their lives are satisfying. *Discipline* includes the tone of correction, and reminds us that finding Wisdom is often not without the pain of making mistakes and having to start again. Education sometimes includes chastisement. *Understanding* carries the sense of 'discernment', and focuses on the rational recognition of right and wrong as well as a practical acceptance of God's truth as the rule of life. *Prudence* for *the simple* (which probably means the inexperienced, the naïve, even the 'gormless'; those whose minds are easily led), is that side of Wisdom which involves shrewd judgments, and cleverness. *Knowledge* and *insight* involve the power of making plans and deciding on the best procedures for achieving one's goal. *Learning* means getting a grasp on what the teacher wishes to convey, and *guidance*[18] is related to a nautical term used for 'rope', with connotations of steering. Sometimes it is used in Proverbs of God's counsel, the steering power of his guidance. Here it suggests that by discovering God's Wisdom, people find that God directs the setting of their sails, and steers their 'boat' on an appropriate course.

As we shall see, the education which the wise teacher offers includes a very large slice of learning from experience. The book of Proverbs is filled with illustrations from everyday life. We are taken into the home (*e.g.* 31:10–11), into the context of friendships (*e.g.* 18:24), into the marketplace and the world of business (*e.g.* 1:20; 11:1); we meet various animals and plants as illustrations of ordinary life (*e.g.* 6:6; 7:22–23; 30:19). Again and again Proverbs says to us: 'Isn't life like this?' It is by reflecting on what actually makes for the best in human life and social relationships, and believing that God wants human beings to flourish, that the wise are able to pass on to others what they have discovered. As we shall also see, the moral education which Proverbs offers is closely related to a sense that this world is an ordered creation of a wise God. The order of the world, as the psalmist also found (*cf.* Ps. 19), is reflected in the moral order which ensures human flourishing. The theologian Edmond Jacob put it like this: 'Wisdom which reigns in nature, should also preside over God's directing of human life.'[19]

Proverbs 1:6 indicates some of the variety of literary devices we shall discover in the book of Proverbs. *Proverbs* (*e.g.* 1:7), *parables* (*e.g.* 6:6–9), *sayings* (*e.g.* 24:14) and *riddles* (*e.g.* 30:18–19) are all part of the armoury by which the wise man confronts his hearers with the truth about their world or themselves. 'Is it not like this?' he seems to say. 'If the world is like this, how then should you live?'

Different parts of the book of Proverbs use different literary forms. R. B. Y. Scott finds at least half a dozen patterns in which this

---

[18] *Cf.* Toy, p. 8.
[19] E. Jacob, *Theology of the Old Testament* (Hodder, 1955), p. 119.

folk wisdom is expressed, and these next paragraphs draw on his suggestions.[20] It is worth remarking also how many of the proverbs rely on humour. The sluggard who lies in bed when there is a lion outside his window (22:13) and the quarrelling spouse who is compared to a dripping tap (27:15) are meant to make us laugh!

One set of patterns points to what we may call *identity* or *equivalence*. Sayings of this sort state: 'This is really identical with, or equivalent to, that.' In Proverbs 14:4, for example, 'Where there are no oxen, the manger is empty' simply says graphically that hard work by oxen is needed to produce food. No oxen means no food. A wise farmer will make sure that there are enough healthy oxen.

A second proverb pattern is *non-identity, contrast* or *paradox*. 'Not every instance of this is that.' As the Prince of Morocco finds written on the scroll in his casket, 'All that glisters is not gold.'[21] In the book of Proverbs, we read that 'a gentle tongue can break a bone' (25:15), and 'to the hungry even what is bitter tastes sweet' (27:7). There is a surprise in this word pattern which makes us sit up and take notice.

Thirdly, the book of Proverbs frequently uses *similarities* or *analogies*, ways of saying, 'This is *like* that.' A whole range of rich analogies is used to face the reader with the reality of human experience. For example: 'Like an ear-ring of gold or an ornament of fine gold is a wise man's rebuke to a listening ear. Like the coolness of snow at harvest time is a trustworthy messenger to those who send him . . . Like clouds and wind without rain is a man who boasts of gifts he does not give' (Pr. 25:12–14).

The fourth pattern focuses on what is *contrary to right order* and is therefore futile or absurd. There is a mocking tone to some of the proverbs, such as 1:17: 'How useless to spread a net in full view of all the birds!' or 17:16: 'Of what use is money in the hand of a fool, since he has no desire to get wisdom?'

The fifth style which Scott refers to *classifies* or *characterizes* persons, actions or situations. There are a number of paragraphs in the book of Proverbs which talk about the 'fool' (*e.g.* in chapters 15 and 17); the 'mocker' (see, *e.g.*, 9:7–8; 13:1; 14:6); the 'sluggard' who should learn from the diligence of the ant (6:6); or the 'good wife', whose virtues are extolled in a clever acrostic poem in chapter 31.

The sayings of Agur include a list of various numerical collections. Perhaps the enumerative device, which we find not only in Proverbs but also occasionally in other Hebrew scriptures (*e.g.* Am. 2 and 3; Jb. 5:19; 33:14), is used partly as an aid to the memory. Perhaps it also reflected something of the pattern and order of the world, yet

---

[20] Scott, pp. 3ff.
[21] Shakespeare, *The Merchant of Venice*, Act 2, Scene 7.

also its mystery (three or four?): 'There are three things that are never satisfied, four that never say "Enough!" . . . There are three things that are too amazing for me, four that I do not understand . . .' (Pr. 30:15, 18).

A sixth pattern, which occurs frequently in the later chapters of Proverbs, is the use of *relative value*: 'This is worth more than that', or 'Better this than that.' 'Better to meet a bear robbed of her cubs than a fool in his folly' (17:12); 'better to be poor than a liar' (19:22).

Finally, there is a set of sayings which turn on the *consequences of human character and behaviour*. Thus 'a happy heart makes the face cheerful' (15:13); 'If a man digs a pit he will fall into it; if a man rolls a stone, it will roll back on him' (26:27).

These and other literary devices offer a method of instruction in practical wisdom. As we are invited to reflect on the world and on human experience, we can learn lessons which help us to cope better, to manage our affairs, to avoid making damaging mistakes, to foster better relationships; in summary, to live more in line with God's ways. Through this range of proverbs, parables, sayings and riddles, we are brought face to face with a variety of human situations which point us to lessons in prudence, diligence, hard work and justice (see Parts 4 and 5). We are admonished to avoid those who despise or deflect us from the wisdom of God, such as the fool and the sluggard and the scoffer (see Part 2). We are warned against the sexual enticements of prostitutes and against the invitation to go with the gang in their violent pursuit of easy pickings. We discover the preciousness of friendship, and yet the ways friends can wound each other. We are confronted with the power for good and for evil of the spoken word. Aspects of marriage and family life are a common theme to bring home to us the meaning of commitment, service and love. Through it all run the themes of God's wisdom as the ordering pattern for the good life, and the ever-present domination of death which sets a limit to life in this world.

We shall begin our detailed study first by drawing out more fully the portrait of wisdom gradually uncovered for us in the first nine chapters of the book of Proverbs. We shall explore the way Wisdom instructs her pupils, and some of the distractions which get in the way. Then we will stand back from the text of Proverbs for an exploration of Wisdom's methods. This will take us into literature, style, approaches education and Wisdom's imagination. Then we move on to the longest section of the book of Proverbs: a series of collections of sayings which we shall use as a way of trying to search out the values on which the wise based their teaching: we shall call this 'Wisdom's Values'. Throughout, we shall try to have a conversation between the wisdom of the wise recorded in these Old Testament chapters, and the wisdom of God made fully known to us in Christ. There may very well be details of life and experience depicted in the book of Proverbs which are so far from everyday life and experience at the dawn of the third millennium that we wonder why we are reading this now. But we shall see that beneath the sayings and the riddles there are values embedded – Wisdom's values – which are as fresh and powerful today as ever. In our task as Christians coming to know God, we will need to think out what expression such values need to have in our lives, if we, in our day, are to live in line with that same wisdom which underlies Proverbs and is most clearly seen in Jesus Christ.

We conclude this chapter by returning to the text on which the book of Proverbs hangs:

> *The fear of the LORD is the beginning of knowledge,*
> *but fools despise wisdom and discipline* (1:7).

This is not an exhortation or a command, an example or a riddle, but simply a statement of fact. *Fear*, of course, here means 'reverent obedience'. It is in reverent obedience to the Lord that all true knowledge finds its controlling principle. This is the *beginning* of wisdom, or rather its 'foremost and essential element' (Toy). It is not a 'beginning' in the sense that it is something we start with and then leave behind. Toy and Kidner both describe this verse as a motto for the wisdom writings in general. The point is that all true knowledge of God, his world and his ways, derives from and is controlled by reverent obedience to God himself as he makes himself known. As David Hubbard helpfully puts it:

Although [fear] includes worship, it does not end there. It radiates out from our adoration and devotion to our everyday conduct that sees each moment as the Lord's time, each relationship as the Lord's opportunity, each duty as the Lord's command, and each blessing as the Lord's gift. It is a new way of looking at life and seeing what it is meant to be when viewed from God's perspective.[22]

> Teach me, my God and King,
>   In all things thee to see,
> And what I do in anything,
>   To do it as for thee!
>
> A man that looks on glass,
>   On it may stay his eye;

[22] Hubbard, p. 48.

Or if he pleaseth, through it pass,
   And then the heaven espy.

All may of thee partake;
   Nothing can be so mean,
Which with his tincture, 'for thy sake',
   Will not grow bright and clean.

A servant with this clause
   Makes drudgery divine:
Who sweeps a room, as for thy laws,
   Makes that and the action fine.

This is the famous stone
   That turneth all to gold;
For that which God doth touch and own
   Cannot for less be told.

George Herbert (1593–1633)

Part 1
Wisdom's portrait (1:1 – 9:18)

The first nine chapters of the book of Proverbs provide us with various sketches of Wisdom. We will examine these in the following pages. Wisdom is no abstract concept; wisdom is personified: she is described as a woman. In some places she is depicted by just a line drawing, one or two of her features emphasized for a particular purpose. In others, we are given a richly coloured, almost three-dimensional portrait. Taken together, these sketches introduce us to a woman who speaks the wisdom of God, and who points the way of life.

This personification of Wisdom is not a (mere) literary device; it reflects the essential nature of biblical wisdom. Wisdom is embodied. Wisdom is for living. In fact, nothing is truly *known* until it is lived out in the everyday world.

It is not until Proverbs 8 that Wisdom's full beauty is described. But throughout the earlier chapters, details of her portrait are being filled in, rather like earlier sketches of a great Renaissance painter. In some art galleries you can see the 'cartoons' – preliminary sketches – of the great works of art, in which the artist has concentrated on one detail or another which will eventually contribute to the finished portrait. Proverbs 1 – 7 gives us a number of preliminary sketches of Wisdom, before her full-colour portrait appears in chapter 8.

These earlier sketches emphasize different aspects of Wisdom's role. Professor Robert Coughenour has drawn together a number of different wisdom themes from the Scriptures, many of which we find illustrated in the first nine chapters of Proverbs. The following paragraphs draw on and adapt his work.[1] We will select, in this

---

[1] I am very grateful to Professor Robert Coughenour of Western Theological Seminary, Holland, Michigan, USA, for his friendship and conversation, and for sending me some of his unpublished work on wisdom literature, as well as drawing my attention to some of his published writings. *Cf.* here the summary in Coughenour, *Perspectives* (September 1990), pp. 4–8, from his other more substantial scholarly works.

chapter, those sections of Proverbs 1 – 9 which fill out Wisdom's portrait, returning to the remaining sections of Proverbs 1 – 9 in our next chapter.

The town crier (1:20–33)

First of all, Wisdom is a sort of town crier, calling aloud at the street corner, making an appeal in the public squares. This is not the ridiculous figure with the billboard so much as the experienced orator at Speakers' Corner, calling to the crowds to take stock of their foolish ways before it is too late. This is, in fact, far more ordinary than Speakers' Corner. In Old Testament social life, we often find that *the gateways of the city* (1:21) are the places where the elders of the city gather to make plans, to enact justice, and to deliberate together about the welfare of the city. In the book of Ruth, it is at the gate that Boaz transacts his business (Ru. 4:1). In the book of Amos (*cf.* 5:15), the leaders are admonished because they have failed to enact justice at the gate. It is here at the city gate that Wisdom issues her call. Wisdom belongs at the centre of public life. She is a brave, passionate woman, with something very serious to say. Hers is a summons to the people to understand. Wisdom reproves those who will not listen, laughs at those who ignore her advice, but offers safety and security to those who heed her call.

Proverbs 1:20–33 is a three-part poem. In the first part (20–23), Wisdom is introduced as calling *aloud in the street, in the public squares*, and *in the gateways*. She calls to the *simple* (naïve) *ones*, asking why they seem to despise wisdom, and asking them to listen to her. Then (24–31) she denounces them, using the past tense for dramatic effect, as though her hearers had already rejected her appeal; and she warns of the *calamity* to come. Verses 24–27 addresses directly those who are mocking, perhaps heckling as she speaks. But Wisdom will have the last *laugh* (26). Then, perhaps turning to the wider crowd of onlookers, she points to her hecklers and comments on their fate (28–31). Verse 28 powerfully reverses the way that God's response to prayerful people is expressed in some other places (contrast, for example, Is. 65:24). Finally, in the third part of the poem (32–33), Wisdom sums up her message: the waywardness of those who ignore wisdom will be their destruction, but there is a more hopeful fate for the attentive.

> Wisdom calls aloud in the street,
> she raises her voice in the public squares;
> ²¹at the head of the noisy streets she cries out,
> in the gateways of the city she makes her speech:
> ²²'How long will you simple ones love your simple ways?

31

> *How long will mockers delight in mockery*
>   *and fools hate knowledge?*
> ²³*If you had responded to my rebuke,*
>   *I would have poured out my heart to you*
>   *and made my thoughts known to you.*
> ²⁴*But since you rejected me when I called*
>   *and no-one gave heed when I stretched out my hand,*
> ²⁵*since you ignored all my advice*
>   *and would not accept my rebuke,*
> ²⁶*I in turn will laugh at your disaster;*
>   *I will mock when calamity overtakes you –*
> ²⁷*when calamity overtakes you like a storm,*
>   *when disaster sweeps over you like a whirlwind,*
>   *when distress and trouble overwhelm you.*
>
> ²⁸*'Then they will call to me but I will not answer;*
>   *they will look for me but will not find me.*
> ²⁹*Since they hated knowledge*
>   *and did not choose to fear the* LORD,
> ³⁰*since they would not accept my advice*
>   *and spurned my rebuke,*
> ³¹*they will eat the fruit of their ways*
>   *and be filled with the fruit of their schemes.*
> ³²*For the waywardness of the simple will kill them,*
>   *and the complacency of fools will destroy them;*
> ³³*but whoever listens to me will live in safety*
>   *and be at ease, without fear of harm.'*

Wisdom offers her advice in the public place. This is no secret knowledge, no private religious opinion. Wisdom can be found, and her advice heard, in the public realm. In the ordinary everyday places where people live their lives, build their relationships, learn their skills, seek their health and defend against death, there God's Wisdom can be heard. So Wisdom faces her hearers with a challenge. There are choices to be made. There is the way of folly, of refusing the reverent obedience to God which is Wisdom's hallmark: the end of that road is deafness, deadness and disaster. Or there is Wisdom's way, bringing the public realm, the choices, and the importance of evaluating between different priorities and different paths, into the light of God. Wisdom offers the life-giving knowledge of God and his ways: how long will the fools hate this knowledge?

Wisdom needs to be searched for (2:1–9)

The second preliminary sketch of Wisdom is rather different. Now she is portrayed not only as one of the disclosures of God's presence in the world, but as someone who sometimes hides, and her treasures need to be searched for. Her standing at the gate is not a strategy for coercing her hearers. She comes over now more as enticing than exhorting. She needs to be sought after and looked for, like a *treasure* as rare as *silver*. The summons to hear Wisdom is really a summons to hear God. The hearers are called to discern God's presence in the world, and give attention to it, not only in the special times, or when God is, so to speak, 'public', but at all times, even when God is hidden. I think it was Jean-Pierre de Caussade (1675–1751)[2] who gave classic expression to the idea which has been captured more recently in the phrase 'the sacrament of the present moment', but the thought is there in the writings of the wise sages of the Old Testament. They had a sense that God was present at all times and his hand could be discerned in all things, when things were going well, as well as in the darkness when God seemed to be absent. God's Wisdom, so to speak, infiltrates all things, but she often needs to be looked for. Wisdom must be sought out. When she is found, her presence provides a *shield* of security, a protection for life's journey.

Separating out verses 1–9 from the rest of Proverbs 2 breaks into a long Hebrew sentence, but these verses highlight this emphasis about Wisdom's elusiveness. It is worth noticing the verbs which are used in the first half of this section: *accept* (1), *store up* (1), *turning your ear* (2), *applying your heart* (2), *call out* (3), *cry aloud* (3), *look for* (4), *search for* (4). These are linked with various phrases beginning *if*. In verses 5–9, we have the responses. *If* this (1–4), *then* this (5–9): *then you will understand* (5, 9) and *find* (5).

> *My son, if you accept my words*
>   *and store up my commands within you,*
> [2]*turning your ear to wisdom*
>   *and applying your heart to understanding,*
> [3]*and if you call out for insight*
>   *and cry aloud for understanding,*
> [4]*and if you look for it as for silver*
>   *and search for it as for hidden treasure,*
> [5]*then you will understand the fear of the LORD*
>   *and find the knowledge of God.*
> [6]*For the LORD gives wisdom,*

[2] Jean-Pierre de Caussade, *Self-Abandonment to Divine Providence* (Collins Fontana, 1971); *e.g.* 'The duties of each moment are shadows beneath which the divine action lies concealed' (p. 32); 'The whole essence of the spiritual life consists in recognising the designs of God for us at the present moment' (p. 38); 'There is no moment at which God does not present himself under the guise of some suffering, some consolation, or some duty' (p. 50).

> *and from his mouth come knowledge and understanding.*
> [7] *He holds victory in store for the upright,*
>   *he is a shield to those whose walk is blameless,*
> [8] *for he guards the course of the just*
>   *and protects the way of his faithful ones.*
>
> [9] *Then you will understand what is right and just*
>   *and fair – every good path.*

With our minds we can come to understand something of God's wisdom, but we need to search for it. When we do, we discover that wisdom is God's precious gift. God is the source of all wisdom; all knowledge comes from God. It is when human beings live in tune with the ways of God that the precious gift of humanity itself is safeguarded and protected.

One of the protections which the way of Wisdom offers is against injustice. She guards 'the paths of justice' (8, RSV). We need to be careful here not to import western concepts of justice into this Hebrew word. Sometimes for us 'justice' has come to mean little more than 'civic fair dealing'. The justice of God which we find referred to throughout the Old Testament includes this meaning, but brings it within a much larger picture. God's justice is to do with the right way of life which God – by royal decree – has revealed. God's justice is God's 'truth to be lived out'. Its essence is captured by Deuteronomy 5:33: 'Walk in all the way that the LORD your God has commanded you, so that you may live and prosper and prolong your days in the land that you shall possess.' Justice also becomes redemptive. Isaiah speaks of 'a righteous God and a Saviour' (Is. 45:21); God's justice merges into his righteousness and goodness on the one hand, and his mercy and steadfast love on the other. When Wisdom 'guards the path of justice', we can include in that path the social justice which demands equity of opportunity and resources for all people within God's world, but we must also broaden the path to lead us to the will of God for righteous living, based on his goodness and his mercy. When you follow Wisdom's way, *you will understand what is right and just and fair* (9); her way leads to what is *good*. These are some of the key themes which later chapters of Proverbs illustrate.

A winsome personality (2:10–15)

Thirdly, Wisdom has a winsome, attractive, womanly personality. She is a delight to know. She shares her life with us in a way that is joyous, affirming, and life-giving.

One key word in these six verses is *pleasant* (10). It is related to the earlier word about wisdom 'entering' the heart, and is to do with the protection Wisdom provides against evil ways. It is part of Wisdom's winsome personality that she wins her way into a person's heart and mind – and that in itself protects (11), guards (11) and saves (12).

> For wisdom will enter your heart,
>   and knowledge will be pleasant to your soul.
> ¹¹Discretion will protect you,
>   and understanding will guard you.
>
> ¹²Wisdom will save you from the ways of wicked men,
>   from men whose words are perverse,
> ¹³who leave the straight paths
>   to walk in dark ways,
> ¹⁴who delight in doing wrong
>   and rejoice in the perverseness of evil,
> ¹⁵whose paths are crooked
>   and who are devious in their ways.

There is, we must note, a recognition in the later verses of this paragraph that all is not well. There is sin in the world and there is stupidity and laziness. Human beings can do dreadful and destructive things to each other; there are those *whose words are perverse* and whose *delight* is *in doing wrong*. But when Wisdom enters your heart (10) and becomes part of your intellectual and moral being, this is *pleasant*: there is a harmony between your soul and God's creation, and your whole humanity is affirmed. Wisdom, in other words, makes you feel good, at home in the world, and safe under the protection of God. We sometimes hear, in political commentary, about the elusive 'feel-good factor', which is meant to be the test of whether the Government is succeeding, the economy is booming, the future is hopeful, and so on. 'Feel-good factor' is in fact a very apt description of what Proverbs suggests the results of seeking Wisdom should be. To be in touch with God, live in God's ways and follow his just paths – in other words for Wisdom to come into your heart – is to produce the sense of security, protection, deliverance and hope which enables us to 'feel good' in God's presence and in God's world. Wisdom is here at one with the writer of Genesis 1, who tells us that God's response to the whole created order, and humankind within it, was, in effect: 'This is good, this is very good.'

Wisdom celebrates life (3:13–18)

A fourth theme picks up on the previous point and develops it.

35

Wisdom is a woman who celebrates life. Proverbs includes this tone of celebration, even of worship, which suggests that life is intended to be lived in all its fullness, and Wisdom is pointing the way.

Blessed is the person who finds Wisdom! This opening phrase of this wonderful short poem which celebrates Wisdom speaks of her as *more profitable* even *than silver* or *gold, more precious* even *than rubies.* This is because her rewards are longer-lasting: *long life* (16), *riches and honour* (16), *pleasant ways* (17), *peace* (17) and a happy life, or a long life (which is probably the main meaning here of *a tree of life,* 18). All those who lay hold of her will be blessed.

> *Blessed is the man who finds wisdom,*
>   *the man who gains understanding,*
> ¹⁴*for she is more profitable than silver*
>   *and yields better returns than gold.*
> ¹⁵*She is more precious than rubies;*
>   *nothing you desire can compare with her.*
> ¹⁶*Long life is in her right hand;*
>   *in her left hand are riches and honour.*
> ¹⁷*Her ways are pleasant ways,*
>   *and all her paths are peace.*
> ¹⁸*She is a tree of life to those who embrace her;*
>   *those who lay hold of her will be blessed.*

This little poem is a sort of hymn in praise of Wisdom. It is rather different from anything we have met so far. Its style is more like Job 28 than much of the rest of Proverbs. Around the poem are sections of instruction, introduced by 'my son' (3:1, 11, 21). Perhaps the editor has placed this poem here to emphasize the link between the teaching of the wisdom schools and Wisdom herself. She, the Wisdom of God himself, is the centre of their teaching.

Earlier we referred to Thomas Traherne, a seventeenth-century English poet who perhaps more than most has celebrated God's creation and the thrill of human life in God's world.

> Your enjoyment of the world is never right, till every morning you awake in Heaven; see yourself in your Father's Palace; and look upon the skies, the earth and the air as Celestial Joys: having such a reverend esteem of all, as if you were among the Angels. The bride of a monarch, in her husband's chamber, hath no such causes of delight as you.³

The Christian church has not always been clear enough about its

³ Thomas Traherne, *Centuries* I. 28.

celebration of God's world. Whatever else William Blake may have meant, there is a pointed warning in his description of the way the 'priests in black gowns were walking their rounds, and binding with briars my joys and desires'.[4]

But Wisdom is here (18) likened to a *tree* which produces *life*; perhaps the phrase means the source of long life and peace. Elsewhere in the Bible we have met the tree of life (*cf.* Gn. 2:9). In that unhappy story, the man and the woman eat the fruit of the other tree. If only they had taken hold of the tree of life instead of listening to the seductions of the serpent! However, the story does not end with their banishment from the tree of life (Gn. 3:22); the life-giving tree is still on offer to those who find God's Wisdom. It is the tree which still yields its fruit and bears its leaves, by the side of the river of the water of life in the heavenly Jerusalem (Rev. 22:2). There the leaves of the tree are for the healing of the nations. Here in Proverbs 3, the fruit of Wisdom's tree sustains, delights and blesses those who find it. Life is a treasure to be celebrated. All Wisdom's *paths are peace*, wholeness, health, contentedness – not only in our inner heart, but also in our outward network of relationships in the world.

The LORD, we learn elsewhere in the Old Testament, is Peace (Jdg. 6:24). Peace is often associated with the coming of Messiah's kingdom (Is. 9:5ff.). But peace is not only the absence of hostilities, not simply the ending of war, and the burning of the warrior's boot. The kingdom of peace is established and upheld 'with justice and with righteousness' (Is. 9:7). The Hebrew word is *šālôm*, which includes everything God gives for human well-being in all areas of life. When the LORD gives shalom there is prosperity (Ps. 72:1–7), health (Is. 57:19), conciliation (Gn. 26:29) and contentedness (Gn. 15:15; Ps. 4:8). When the shalom of the LORD is present, there are good relationships between nations and between people (1 Ch. 12:17–18). There is both a personal and a social dimension. 'Seek the [shalom] of the city where I have sent you into exile,' says God through Jeremiah, 'and pray to the LORD on its behalf, for in its [shalom] you will find your [shalom]' (Je. 29:7, RSV). Shalom, then, is about the enjoyment and blessing of right relationships, with God, with neighbour, with oneself, and with one's environment. There is no shalom without righteousness and justice. Blessing, profit, preciousness, riches, honour, life, pleasantness, peace: these are the gifts of Wisdom to the person who finds her. Human life in this world is to be affirmed, celebrated and enjoyed, and Wisdom points the way.

---

4 'The Garden of Love'.

Wisdom likes to explore (4:1–9)

This paragraph takes the portrait of Wisdom a stage further. The wise man is teaching his son (1–5), but then his instruction slips over into praise of Wisdom (4:6–9).

The paragraph begins rather like the introduction to some of the other instruction sections. The father urges his *sons* to *pay attention* (1), and then thinks back to his own upbringing (3–4), before commending Wisdom (5) and elaborating on her rewards (6–9).

> *Listen, my sons, to a father's instruction;*
> *pay attention and gain understanding.*
> ²*I give you sound learning,*
> *so do not forsake my teaching.*
> ³*When I was a boy in my father's house,*
> *still tender, and an only child of my mother,*
> ⁴*he taught me and said,*
> *'Lay hold of my words with all your heart;*
> *keep my commands and you will live.*
> ⁵*Get wisdom, get understanding;*
> *do not forget my words or swerve from them.*
> ⁶*Do not forsake wisdom, and she will protect you;*
> *love her, and she will watch over you.*
> ⁷*Wisdom is supreme; therefore get wisdom.*
> *Though it cost all you have, get understanding.*
> ⁸*Esteem her, and she will exalt you;*
> *embrace her, and she will honour you.*
> ⁹*She will set a garland of grace on your head*
> *and present you with a crown of splendour.'*

It is worth pausing on the first four verses, which fit into the general Old Testament pattern of education within families. Parents were expected to show the concern, intimacy, and authority which made their instructions life-giving for their children. As Deuteronomy put it in relation to God's commandments: 'These commandments that I give you today are to be upon your hearts. Impress them on your children. Talk about them when you sit at home . . .' (Dt. 6:6–7). Parenting includes the responsibility of exercising the sort of authority which enables growth to maturity. It is an authority which gives freedom for the pupil to 'get wisdom, get insight'. It is not an authority which stifles exploration and discovery.[5]

Indeed, one of the points which this paragraph makes very clear,

---

[5] *Cf. e.g.* David Atkinson, *Pastoral Ethics* (Lynx, 1994), ch. 6: 'The Future of the Family'.

though it was present also in 3:13ff., is that the path to Wisdom is precisely one of openness, inquisitiveness, exploration and discovery. The verbs here are *gain, lay hold of, keep, get, love, esteem, embrace*. Wisdom is worth searching for. And the reward for the search, and for loyalty shown to Wisdom once you have found her, is that *she will set a garland of grace on your head and present you with a crown of splendour*, perhaps such as you might wear at a wedding. Your life will be ennobled and enriched if you get Wisdom, for she will honour your loyalty to her. Be open, then, to her words and her ways. This is a warning against closed minds, tunnel vision and parochialism. Wisdom's call crosses barriers of race and nationality (*cf.* 8:4). None is excluded from her gifts except the fool and the mocker and those who refuse her offer. But those who find her will be those who have searched, open-minded, and with a longing to learn.

These five sketches have drawn on specific paragraphs from Proverbs, and we have printed the text along with each sketch. The next two sections stand back a little from the whole sweep of chapters 1 – 9, and indicate two other features of Wisdom's character which seem to be indicated in a number of more isolated verses, and which are also referred to in later chapters of Proverbs. They are, however, both important aspects of Wisdom's character: justice and order.

Wisdom stands for justice

Wisdom's character includes a strong streak of justice. To walk in the ways of Wisdom is to walk justly. Her ethic is an ethic of justice, an invitation to and a requirement for justice. In many of the detailed proverbs later in the book we will find an underlying assumption of the importance of justice. Here in these opening nine chapters, Wisdom's ways are seen to be 'paths of justice' (8:20).

Earlier we remarked on the importance of understanding the word 'justice' in terms of the whole will and command of God for right living. God's justice merges into his righteousness and goodness, and into his mercy and love. But justice includes social equity. In the very first chapter we read that the attainment of wisdom concerned 'doing what is right and just and fair' (1:3). This was repeated in 2:9. In chapter 8, Wisdom says that by her, 'kings reign and rulers make laws that are just' (8:15). However, Wisdom's ethic is expressed rather differently from the command ethic of the law books in the Pentateuch, and from some of the Old Testament prophets. Wisdom's call to justice is more subtle. She does not operate predominantly with an ethic of rules, laws to be obeyed and codes to be adopted. Wisdom's morality is broader than a morality of law; her justice is more personal than merely fairness. She describes justice by describing life's experiences in parables and riddles, and invites the readers to put their own lives beside them. She seems to say: 'Here is an illustration of justice; now you judge yourselves in the light of it. This is the way of righteousness; do you match up?' For example, Wisdom is concerned with the plight of the poor: 'He who mocks the poor shows contempt for their Maker' (17:5). She is concerned with honesty in business: 'The LORD abhors dishonest scales, but accurate weights are his delight' (11:1). She insists that the administration of justice must be absolutely above board. 'It is not good to be partial to the wicked or to deprive the innocent of justice' (18:5). Wisdom paints these pictures for us and then asks us whether our behaviour comes up to standard. Where are we in the pictures? Do we mock the poor – or fail to notice them in the underpass and the doorways? Do we use dishonest weights, or make dishonest tax returns? Do we show unjust partiality, fail to tell the whole truth, or allow unjust criticism of others to pass unchallenged? The way that leads to life in all its fullness is the way of God, which at its heart is God's righteousness and justice. Wisdom asks us: 'Do you live like that?'

Wisdom likes things ordered

The search for Wisdom is more generally a search for order. The figure of Wisdom calling at the street corner (1:20) breathes a sense of confidence in the world. She urges an openness to the world, and she says to her hearers, in effect: 'You are part of this world and need to take a responsible share in it.' The confidence she shows is based on the fundamental assumption that this is an ordered world. There is a great deal in the book of Proverbs which instructs the readers in the ordered life. Later in this book we will explore many of the contrasts between 'the righteous' and 'the wicked'. But in these opening chapters this theme is introduced. The search for order includes integrity (10:9), instruction (10:17) and good sense (13:15). Robert Coughenour comments: 'Whatever that order is called, it is a confession of faith that life is good, that health and wholeness are possible, and that right relations in a community are a wise way of living.' In other words, when as Christian people we take wisdom thinking seriously, we are open to the contexts in which we are set, and within which we can celebrate and enjoy life.

For the covenant people of God in the Old Testament, that culture was of course very different from post-Enlightenment western culture. Our social patterns, assumptions and priorities are in many ways very different from theirs. We no less than they, however, need to develop social cultures in which to grow – families, communities, churches and so on. Wisdom tells us that for good living, these 'cultures to grow in' need to reflect the values and order and character of God. She also reminds us that we need to be open to learn from and receive from others in our world. God's order is seen not only in our family or our church. We learn of his wisdom also by being open to others. The book of Proverbs itself illustrates this in the extent to which some of the text seems to draw on and adapt wisdom teaching from others outside the family of God. There is nothing about the world from which we should hide, come apart and be separate, except the foolishness, laziness and contempt for God's ways which refuse to hear the voice of Wisdom.

Wisdom illustrates the pattern of creation (3:19–20)

Underlying all that has been said about the richness of human life and the order of the world is a fundamental theology of creation. True Wisdom is the wisdom of God the creator. Other parts of the Old Testament make much of God as lawgiver and as redeemer. These themes are present in Proverbs, but the wise men talked more about God as creator of the world. And now the portrait of Wisdom becomes transposed itself into something richer and fuller. For Wisdom is now not only the voice at the street corner and at the city gates, calling to the people to follow the ways of God the creator. She is not only the attractive woman who offers life-giving blessing; nor only the woman who sometimes hides and who needs to be searched for. Wisdom herself is seen in fact to be the ordered principle of creation itself. Let us go back now to some key verses we left on one side in chapter 3.

In verses 19–20 of chapter 3, following on the little hymn which praises wisdom without any explicit reference to God (3:13–18), what we now find emphasized is that it is Yahweh who is at the creative centre of all things (19). Wisdom comes from God, an instrument in his creative work, yet far superior to all other created things, as she was there even before the world was made. Wisdom is Yahweh's wisdom.

> *By wisdom the* LORD *laid the earth's foundations,*
>   *by understanding he set the heavens in place;*
> *20by his knowledge the deeps were divided,*
>   *and the clouds let drop the dew.*

Perhaps these verses were once an independent saying. The focus of attention is not so much Wisdom as Yahweh himself. The emphasis is on the LORD. Wisdom here is his instrument, a tool in his hand.

41

The Wisdom we are coming to know through these different sketches is the wisdom of Yahweh himself. This is the same picture we find elaborated more in chapter 8, and also in the majestic poem to Wisdom in Job 28. In Job's context, Professor Frances Young's descriptive phrase seems most apt: Wisdom is the Wild Order of Things.[6]

Proverbs perhaps talks more about Wisdom's beauty than her wildness, but both Proverbs and Job face us with the awesome beauty, the creative wildness, the underlying order of all things. God's creative work is used to illustrate his greatness and his care for people. Toy's commentary contrasts this perspective of Wisdom's skill in the whole of creation with other concerns expressed in other creation poems: the social interest in Genesis 2, and reassurance for the people of their place in the world as God's people, which underlies Genesis 1. Wisdom is the divine direction of the whole material world.

Proverbs 3:19–20 is set in the middle of a chapter of instructions about right living. The person who finds wisdom – the person who is in tune with God's creative purposes for the world, and who lives in the light of God's ordering of the world – will truly live. To quote Hubbard once more:

> The argument is clear: if Yahweh with wisdom as His tool could accomplish the wonders of the various phases of creation – setting the earth on its foundations, setting the heavens in their appointed place, breaking up the depths to irrigate the dry land through wells, springs and streams, and watering the earth with dew from the clouds, think what wisdom will do . . . what Yahweh will do through wisdom in the lives of those who find it.[7]

The way of wisdom, despite the human perversity which threatens God's created goodness, is to live in the light of God's created order. Proverbs gives us many ways of understanding what that means in practical experience. Indeed, in chapter 10 onwards there is a wealth of practical examples of what good living amounts to in various contexts. Here in Proverbs 3 we are reminded of a more fundamental truth: that all life is held in being and comes to its fulfilment only through the creative power and love of God.

Proverbs is careful also to remind us that this applies not only to human life. We remember that the classic chapter on creation, in Genesis 1, says quite a lot about trees, plants, birds, reptiles, land

---

[6] From her poem 'Sophie's Call', part of which is quoted with permission in David Atkinson, *The Message of Job* (IVP, 1991), p. 129.
[7] Hubbard, p. 75.

animals and so on, before it comes to human beings. All have a place in God's creative purposes. All are part of the world of which God said, 'This is good.' The various writers of Proverbs also recognize that other creatures alongside human beings are part of God's world. The ant can illustrate good management of provisions to the sluggard (Pr. 6:6–8); eagles and snakes draw forth amazement (30:19); the horse (21:31), the badger, the locust, the lizard, the lion, the strutting cock and the he-goat (30:26–31) are all used to make different points. The whole of the created order receives its life from God.

Too often the Christian church is criticized for a faith which, it is said, exalts human life over all other life, and has contributed to the ecological crisis of our time. It is true that the Genesis texts about 'having dominion' have been interpreted by some within the church as giving human beings a divine mandate to exploit the rest of the created order as we wish. The American historian Lynn White Jr has been widely quoted as describing Christianity as 'the most anthropocentric religion the world has seen' and as blaming the medieval church for the current pollution of the environment. By contrast, others have rightly pointed out that it was the commercial incentives arising from the Industrial Revolution which bear the brunt of the blame. And many other Christian writers have made clear that the divine mandate in Genesis is for responsible stewardship of the created order, and that to be made in the divine image includes the responsibility of being God's 'estate manager' for the well-being of all creatures. The writer of Proverbs 12:10 said quite clearly: 'A righteous man cares for the needs of his animal.' And the prophet Hosea (2:18) clearly includes animals within God's covenant purposes.[8] Christians should be at the forefront of the ecological debates, working for a greater understanding and honouring of the whole of the inhabited earth, and of the welfare of animals within it. The way of Wisdom is the art of steering a course through the times and places of life, in line with the creative order of God, for the well-being of the whole of his creation.

The full-colour portrait (8:1–31)

It is Proverbs 8 which brings the portrait of Wisdom and her ways to its climax, and we do well to consider this in some detail, as it holds together much that we have already said. This marvellous chapter, described by one commentator as 'the summit of Old Testament discipleship',[9] begins with Wisdom's elaborate and extended call for

---

[8] See Keith Thomas, *Man and the Natural World: Changing Attitudes in England 1500–1800* (Penguin, 1983), pp. 22ff.

[9] Hubbard, p. 117.

attention (1–11), which leads into a paragraph on the values and advantages of following Wisdom's way (12–21), and then a majestic celebration of Wisdom's authority as God's creation partner (22–31). The chapter ends with a final plea for attention (32–36).

The personification of Wisdom as a woman crying out for people to listen to her call reaches its fullest expression in this chapter. The portrait of Wisdom as a woman began in 1:20–33 and was also glanced at in 7:4. But here the colours are painted in more richly.

We look first at verses 1–11. As with other speeches from Wisdom, the address is to the *simple* (naïve) ones (5), but it is also here *to all mankind* (4). The message is the same. Wisdom calls (1, 4, 6). She says important things for your benefit (5, 6, 7). The rewards of paying attention are great (9, 10, 11).

> *Does not wisdom call out?*
> *Does not understanding raise her voice?*
> ²*On the heights along the way,*
> *where the paths meet, she takes her stand;*
> ³*beside the gates leading into the city,*
> *at the entrances, she cries aloud:*
> ⁴*"To you, O men, I call out;*
> *I raise my voice to all mankind.*
> ⁵*You who are simple, gain prudence;*
> *you who are foolish, gain understanding.*
> ⁶*Listen, for I have worthy things to say;*
> *I open my lips to speak what is right.*
> ⁷*My mouth speaks what is true,*
> *for my lips detest wickedness.*
> ⁸*All the words of my mouth are just;*
> *none of them is crooked or perverse.*
> ⁹*To the discerning all of them are right;*
> *they are faultless to those who have knowledge.*
> ¹⁰*Choose my instruction instead of silver,*
> *knowledge rather than choice gold,*
> ¹¹*for wisdom is more precious than rubies,*
> *and nothing you desire can compare with her.*

Iris Murdoch follows Simone Weil in saying that moral and personal change is not something which comes about just by an exercise of will, but by *giving attention* to the world around us. The will 'only controls a few movements of a few muscles . . . Attention is something quite different . . . Attention, taken to its highest degree, is the same thing as prayer . . . Absolutely unmixed attention is prayer . . . Attention is bound up with desire – or, more exactly, consent.'[10] Murdoch goes on to say: 'There is something about the human spirit which seems to some thinkers to *demand* a search for "deep foundations".'

Wisdom, then, is calling for attention, for a committed search for those deep foundations, for consent to the ways of God in the world. She stands in the open places, in the public realm, and calls for our allegiance.

Unlike the other woman who makes herself very obvious in the opening chapters of Proverbs, namely the seductress who 'lurks' behind the corners (7:12), trying to entice the unwary to her bed, Wisdom stands in the open places, *on the heights* (perhaps highways or thoroughfares), at the crossroads, by the city *gates*. Wisdom makes herself known where people meet and talk. There is nothing furtive, nothing underhand, about Wisdom.

> There is the beauty of goodness in all that she says; there is the charming directness and openness of truth; she abhors tortuous and obscure ways; and if some of her sayings seem paradoxes or enigmas, a little difficult to understand, that is the fault of the hearer; to a tortuous mind straight things appear crooked; to the ignorant and uninstructed mind the eternal laws of God appear foolishness; but all that she says is plain to one who understands, and right to those who find knowledge.[11]

Wisdom's call (4) is to all humankind. No barriers of race, class, sex or tribal allegiance need prevent Wisdom's voice reaching all people. Wisdom seeks her disciples both from those who are learned, and from those who are *simple*. And she begins her appeal by proclaiming what is *right*, *true* and *just* (6–8). Her words, she claims, are more valuable than the sort of things most people regard as valuable: *silver, choice gold, rubies*. Indeed, *nothing you can desire can compare with her* (11). So her call is for the hearer to *gain prudence* (5) ('true knowledge of the principles of life');[12] to *gain understanding* (5) – that is, to 'have an understanding heart'; and to *listen* (6).

The central thrust of this first paragraph is that before and behind our human searchings after wisdom, Wisdom is searching for us.

The second paragraph (8:12–21) continues an elaboration of Wisdom's virtues and the advantages of paying attention to her. She is a close colleague of *prudence, knowledge and discretion* (12). She is

---

[10] Iris Murdoch, *Metaphysics as a Guide to Morals* (Penguin, 1992), p. 52; *cf.* also Simone Weil, *Gravity and Grace* (1947; Routledge, 1992), pp. 105ff.

[11] Horton, p. 107.

[12] Toy, p. 162.

at home with *counsel and sound judgment* (14). Good rulers are governed by her principles (15–16). Paying attention to her brings life-giving rewards (17–21).

> *'I, wisdom, dwell together with prudence;*
> *I possess knowledge and discretion.*
> ¹³*To fear the LORD is to hate evil;*
> *I hate pride and arrogance,*
> *evil behaviour and perverse speech.*
> ¹⁴*Counsel and sound judgment are mine;*
> *I have understanding and power.*
> ¹⁵*By me kings reign*
> *and rulers make laws that are just;*
> ¹⁶*by me princes govern,*
> *and all nobles who rule on earth.*
> ¹⁷*I love those who love me,*
> *and those who seek me find me.*
> ¹⁸*With me are riches and honour,*
> *enduring wealth and prosperity.*
> ¹⁹*My fruit is better than fine gold;*
> *what I yield surpasses choice silver.*
> ²⁰*I walk in the way of righteousness,*
> *along the paths of justice,*
> ²¹*bestowing wealth on those who love me*
> *and making their treasuries full.'*

Wisdom shares a house with *prudence* (12). This verse could mean that 'wisdom dwells in prudence, or intelligence'. She possesses (or perhaps the translation should be 'has the ability to keep on discovering') *knowledge and discretion* (12). Before telling us of the advantages of her ways, Wisdom points us back again to the fear of the LORD, which Toy understands here primarily as 'moral insight' from God. It shows itself in the hatred of evil and the rejection of perversity. Wisdom hates that which is turned away from the truth.

The upshot of all this is that Proverbs is here indicating that our moral development goes hand in hand with our cognitive development: the moral life and the intellectual life should be inseparable in 'the fear of the LORD'.

True knowledge is never merely the collection of information, any more than science is merely 'tying facts into bundles'. The philosopher of science Michael Polanyi made short shrift of such a positivistic attitude to science when he described it in this way:

No scientist is ever concerned with producing the most convenient summary of a given set of facts. This is the task of the

editors of encyclopaedias and of telephone directories. It is of the
essence of a scientific theory that it commits us to an indetermin-
ate range of yet undreamed consequences that may flow from it.
We commit ourselves to these, because we believe that by our
theory we are making contact with a reality of which our theory
has revealed one aspect.[13]

For Polanyi, knowledge entails commitment; knowledge is
essentially personal. By that he means that when something is
'known', it is known by people with skills, people who make
assumptions, people who read instruments, people who make
decisions, people who judge probabilities, especially people who are
committed. He insists that all knowledge entails commitment. One
of his favourite examples is riding a bicycle. When I tried to teach my
daughter to ride a bicycle, I could explain all about balance, pressure
on the pedals, how to turn the handle bars, and what to do when she
wanted to stop. But it was not until we went out into the school
playground and actually tried that she began to discover, to know,
what riding a bicycle meant. She had to take the risk, make the
commitment of faith, try it out. Knowledge came by participating,
by doing, by taking part. We do not know many things by just
collecting facts, but by committing ourselves in certain beliefs to act
on those beliefs. We know not by detachment, but by participation.
For Polanyi, even the most 'objective' of the sciences, such as
physics, involves an irreducibly personal and moral dimension in its
knowledge. This is not very far from the Wisdom of Proverbs, in
which the fear of the LORD holds moral and intellectual life together.

Then Wisdom begins to outline her values and her powers (14–
18), and the advantages which following her way brings (19–21).

Wisdom offers *counsel and sound judgment, understanding and
power*, and these *riches* are put within everyone's reach. Here we
have the capacity to give good advice coupled with the practical skill
to arrange things to lead to a good outcome, and the power to
achieve it. These abilities flow from *the fear of the LORD*. They are
the capacities people need to make sense of their lives and cope with
life's needs.

Then the attention is focused particularly on one group of people
who need such understanding and skill: the national leaders (15).
Several times in the book of Proverbs, we find attention given to
kings, princes and *rulers*, and perhaps also to the young men who
were being groomed for high office. What these future leaders – and
not only they – need above all is the range of gifts Wisdom can give,
and these are for the establishment of justice (15). The source of

[13] M. Polanyi, 'The Scientific Outlook: Its Sickness and Cure', *Science* (March 1957).

royal achievements is Wisdom. It is interesting to place this insight alongside that of the psalmist: it is God 'who gives victory to kings' (Ps. 144:10).

The heart of Wisdom is caring *love* (17), and her love is not arbitrary. Wisdom loves all who *love* her and *seek* her. Her offer is universal. If any miss out on her gifts, it is because they will not seek her. And the rewards include *riches, honour, wealth, prosperity, righteousness* and *justice*. These are the words often summarized elsewhere in the Old Testament as 'shalom': justice, righteousness and peace within and between peoples and communities – and between people and communities and God. As we discover in 8:35, these are part of the whole gift which Wisdom has to impart, called there 'life . . . favour from the LORD'.

The third paragraph of chapter 8 (22–31) takes us right to the heart of things. Wisdom claims that she was Yahweh's firstborn (22) *before the world began* (23–29). She was not only *the craftsman at his side* (30), but also Yahweh's *delight* (30), sharing his joy in the *whole world* (31).

> 'The LORD brought me forth as the first of his works,
>   before his deeds of old;
> ²³I was appointed from eternity,
>   from the beginning, before the world began.
> ²⁴When there were no oceans, I was given birth,
>   when there were no springs abounding with water;
> ²⁵before the mountains were settled in place,
>   before the hills, I was given birth,
> ²⁶before he made the earth or its fields
>   or any of the dust of the world.
> ²⁷I was there when he set the heavens in place,
>   when he marked out the horizon on the face of the deep,
> ²⁸when he established the clouds above
>   and fixed securely the fountains of the deep,
> ²⁹when he gave the sea its boundary
>   so that the waters would not overstep his command,
>   and when he marked out the foundations of the earth.
> ³⁰Then I was the craftsman at his side.
>   I was filled with delight day after day,
>   rejoicing always in his presence,
> ³¹rejoicing in his whole world
>   and delighting in mankind.'

This autobiographical paragraph stands apart in style and language from the rest of this chapter. This paragraph, perhaps more than anywhere else in the Bible, couples the wonder of God's creation with its excitement, exuberance, exhilaration and delight. There is little that can compare with the excitement we relive if we can look back on some great event, perhaps a royal wedding, the launch of a space shuttle, or the day our team won the Superbowl or the World Cup, and say, 'I was there.' These are Wisdom's words in 8:27: *I was there when* God *set the heavens in place.*

This fine section begins with God: *The LORD brought me forth as the first of his works.* This reads like an extended elaboration of Proverbs 3:19–20. Here we see the intimate relation between the LORD and Wisdom, whom God brought into being before the work of creation began. Wisdom is Yahweh's own. Wisdom can offer knowledge about human life and its ways, she can advise on the government of society and she can give the rewards of health and justice, because from the very beginning she has been at the heart of things; she was present when the world was made. The picture here is of Wisdom as the principle by which God ordered the world; God's firstborn, who was present with God in the world's creation, and the enlightenment of all human life. Our minds are immediately turned back to Genesis 1 and the poem reflecting on the order of God's creation. Our minds are also moved on to the prologue of John's gospel, in which the Logos is described: 'In the beginning was the Word . . .' (Jn. 1:1–4).

In Proverbs 8, the first thought (22–23) is of Wisdom's place in the mind and purpose of God. *The LORD brought me forth* (or the text might better be translated 'possessed me') *as the first of his works, before his deeds of old; I was appointed from eternity, before the world began.* The writer is suggesting that Wisdom was 'brought forth' at a point in time, but whether this means 'created' or 'coeval with the beginning of God's creative work' is not altogether clear. All we are told is that before the beginning of the world, Wisdom was a partner in the life and purpose of God.

The next verses (24–26) describe Wisdom's birth before the creation of the physical world. The picture of *oceans, springs abounding with water, mountains, hills, the earth* and *its fields* and *dust,* recalls the emergence of creation in Genesis 1:6–10. Before any of this happened, says Proverbs, Wisdom was there.

She was thus present as the world was made (27–29). Once again, the setting of *the heavens,* the marking out of a *horizon* for *the deep,* establishing *the clouds* and setting boundaries for the sea, are all reminiscent of the creation poem in Genesis.

And then we come to the climax of this section. Verses 30–31 celebrate Wisdom's joyous delight in being God's intimate associate (which is what *the craftsman at his side* probably means). There is a thrill, a delight, a dance in these verses. *I was filled with delight* could even mean 'I was a source of delight to God'; 'I was God's delight.'

Wisdom is so excited and energized by God's creative work that she 'rejoices' in God's presence, a word which could mean 'sports' or 'laughs'. The poet here is conveying the sense of a little child at play. 'Like a gleeful kid, wisdom is so excited by the majesty and power of the creation, that she jokes and laughs about it daily with the Creator, who takes exquisite delight in her jollity.'[14] That joy is *in his whole world*, and especially *in mankind* (31).

This is a remarkably fresh and vibrant picture of creation. This is more intimately personal than the majestic poem of Genesis 1. This is much more positive and joyous than the struggle among the gods which fills some of the other creation stories of the ancient Near East. This is much more vibrantly alive and hopeful than the evolutionary philosophies which depict the emergence of life as just one thing after another. To follow Wisdom is to follow the way of exuberance, creativity, laughter and joy, what Horton calls 'exultant cheerfulness', or what Thomas Traherne meant when he urged his readers to 'enjoy the world'.

No wonder this picture of Wisdom filled out for the New Testament writers, and notably St Paul, some of what they wanted to say about Jesus, the Christ, the Wisdom of God. There are hints of Wisdom in Colossians 1:15–18, for example:

He is the image of the invisible God, the firstborn over all creation. For by him all things were created: things in heaven and on earth, visible and invisible, whether thrones or powers or rulers or authorities; all things were created by him and for him. He is before all things, and in him all things hold together. And he is the head of the body, the church; he is the beginning and the firstborn from among the dead, so that in everything he might have the supremacy.

W. D. Davies is typical of many in his comment on how both aspects of the twofold function of Wisdom in Proverbs 8 – 9, in the cosmos and in the world of human beings, are transferred to Christ in Paul's discussion in this passage. Christ is depicted not only as creator of the physical universe, but as the agent of the re-creation of humanity.[15] There are hints, too, in the opening of the letter to the Hebrews (1:1–3):

In the past God spoke to our forefathers through the prophets at

[14] Hubbard, p. 125.
[15] W. D. Davies, *Paul and Rabbinic Judaism* (SPCK, 1948), p. 152. *Cf.* N. T. Wright's helpful use of C. F. Burney's work comparing Colossians with Gn. 1 and with Pr. 8 – 9, in Wright's *Colossians and Philemon* (IVP, 1986), p. 67.

many times and in various ways, but in these last days he has spoken to us by his Son, whom he appointed heir of all things, and through whom he made the universe. The Son is the radiance of God's glory and the exact representation of his being, sustaining all things by his powerful word. After he had provided purification for sins, he sat down at the right hand of the Majesty in heaven.

There are more hints, of course, in the opening of the fourth gospel (Jn. 1:1–5):

In the beginning was the Word, and the Word was with God, and the Word was God. He was with God in the beginning.
Through him all things were made; without him nothing was made that has been made. In him was life, and that life was the light of men. The light shines in the darkness, but the darkness has not understood it.

Proverbs 8 was often used by early Christian theologians in the controversies surrounding the discussion of the second Person of the Trinity; it was used by Augustine in his controversy with the Arians. Later Calvin sought to rebutt Servetus' refusal to accept that Jesus Christ was the eternal Son of God by citing this passage: 'the eternal begetting of wisdom of which Solomon speaks is annihilated [in Servetus' account]'. And Matthew Henry applies the passage directly to Jesus:

That it is an intelligent and divine Person that here speaks seems very plain, and that it is not meant of a mere essential property of the divine nature; for wisdom here has personal properties and actions; and that intelligent, divine Person, can be no other than the Son of God himself, to whom the principal things here spoken of wisdom are attributed in other scriptures.

Now there has been considerable controversy as to whether Wisdom in this passage is a true Person, or rather the personification of one of God's attributes. Most commentators take the latter view, and probably the text itself does not allow anything more. However, to read these words of the sages as part of the ongoing self-revelation of God, culminating in the incarnation of Jesus, means that we are not too far off track if we find very close parallels between the character of Wisdom here, and the character of Jesus in the gospels. Indeed, Matthew Henry was right to say: 'The best exposition of these verses we have in the four first verses of St. John's Gospel.'

And how appropriate to understand Jesus in the terms in which Wisdom is described: God's delight! This is perhaps the sense which is captured (though the Hebrew word is different) when Isaiah speaks of God's servant (42:1): 'Here is my servant, whom I uphold, my chosen one in whom I delight.' And this theme is picked up in the narrative of Jesus' baptism, when the heavens open, the Spirit of God descends, and a voice from heaven is heard: 'This is my Son, whom I love; with him I am well pleased' (Mt. 3:17). Jesus is God's delight.

The last paragraph of Proverbs 8 concludes the appeal for attention, and returns to the instructive style with which the chapter began.

> 'Now then, my sons, listen to me;
>   blessed are those who keep my ways.
> [33] Listen to my instruction and be wise;
>   do not ignore it.
> [34] Blessed is the man who listens to me,
>   watching daily at my doors,
>   waiting at my doorway.
> [35] For whoever finds me find life
>   and receives favour from the LORD.
> [36] But whoever fails to find me harms himself;
>   all who hate me love death.'

Now Wisdom resumes her speech with a final call for attention. She has made out her case for why she should be heard. She embodies God's knowledge; she was present when everything else was made. She is God's delight. So now she calls her hearers to *listen*. There is blessing for those who follow Wisdom's way, *watching* and *waiting*. That blessing is described in verse 35 as *life* and as *favour from the LORD*. The sad final truth, however, is that whoever does not seek for Wisdom and find her *harms himself* (36).

Wisdom: her main features

It is time now to stand back from this chapter, and indeed from our exploration so far of these first nine chapters of Proverbs, and draw together some of the main themes.

First, this world does not exist because of some blind chance. Underneath everything that happens is the creative and loving purpose of God. It was the French biochemist Jacques Monod who ended his beautifully written but ultimately despairingly nihilistic book, *Chance and Necessity*, with the words: 'The ancient covenant is in pieces; man at last knows that he is alone in the unfeeling immensity of the universe, out of which he emerged only by chance.'[16]

[16] J. Monod, *Chance and Necessity* (Collins, 1971), p. 167.

That most evangelical of atheists, Professor Richard Dawkins,[17] seems to want to personify Chance, almost as though Chance plays for him the role of God: 'Chance with natural selection, chance smeared out into innumerable tiny steps over aeons of time, is powerful enough to manufacture miracles like dinosaurs and ourselves.'[18] Both of these writers place 'chance' at the heart of all things.

Of course the physical world shows a wonderful interplay of chance and necessity, form and fruitfulness. But Professor John Polkinghorne read Monod's evidence in a wholly different way:

> When I read Monod's book, I was greatly excited by the scientific picture it presented. Instead of seeing the role of chance as an indication of the purposelessness and futility of the world [as Monod does], I was deeply moved by the thought of the astonishing fruitfulness that is revealed inherent in the laws of atomic physics.[19]

Polkinghorne understands the world rather in terms of 'the rationality and faithfulness of God'. Likewise, Wisdom shows us a world at the heart of which can be found the loving, faithful purposes of God.

Secondly, the Wisdom of Proverbs indicates that the order of the world, which we know to be a basic assumption of all scientific endeavour, is an order implanted by God as a reflection of his own nature. He creates the world as an expression of himself, as the outcome of his own design. Our intelligent apprehension of the world depends on some correspondence between our minds and the order of the world out there. That correspondence, we learn from Proverbs 8, can be understood as the work of Wisdom: the principle of creation is made available to our understanding.

This is not far from the statement of Dr Arthur Peacocke:

> The realisation that our minds can find the world intelligible, and the implication this has that an explanation for the world process is to be found in mental rather than purely material categories, has been for many scientists who are theists, including the present writer, an essential turning point in their thinking. Why *should* science work at all? That it does so points strongly to a principle of rationality, to an interpretation of the cosmos in terms of mind

---

[17] *Cf.* his book *The Blind Watchmaker* (Penguin, 1986).
[18] Quoted by Michael Poole in *Science and Belief* (Lion, 1990), p. 124.
[19] J. Polkinghorne, *One World* (SPCK, 1986), p. 54.

as its most significant feature. Any thinking which takes science seriously must, it seems to me, start from this.[20]

He goes on to argue that 'the scientific perspective is a most compelling pointer to God'.[21] Wisdom discloses an ordered world which reflects the mind of God.

Thirdly, Wisdom suggest that the disorders of the world need to be seen in the light of an overriding and joyous purpose. There is much that is stimulating about the new emphasis in so-called 'creation spirituality', popularized by writers such as Matthew Fox.[22] Fox celebrates creation's gifts, especially the gift of awe – a response to creation which leads to transformative action to honour the earth and seek interdependence and justice. There is much here which corresponds with the concerns of Wisdom in Proverbs. However, although Fox speaks about the 'impoverishment of the soul' which especially afflicts the First World, he does not say much about the fallenness of the world, about human sin and the culpable human folly which, Proverbs says, leads to death, or about the need for forgiveness and redemption. 'The fear of the LORD' for Fox becomes 'the awe we feel at being in the universe'. He does not couple it as clearly as Proverbs does with the call not to be 'wise in your own eyes', but to 'shun evil' (3:7). There is less sense, in Fox's writings, of the balance which Proverbs strikes between the call of Wisdom and the call of Folly, and less recognition than there should be of the disorders of the fallen world.

We need to recognize that there is much about this present world which is not joyous, which surely does not give God delight, and which we need to name as 'evil'. Our next chapter illustrates this in Proverbs. There are many detractors from Wisdom's ways, leading to suffering, disillusionment and hardship. Yet we are not to see evil as an equal and opposite power over against God. The world's disorders can often be linked to the aberrations caused by those who do not heed the call of Wisdom, and whose rejection of God's ways is the road to *death* (8:36).

Fourthly, in the very conception of the universe, it seems that God has human life in mind. Wisdom, we find, is God's delight, present at the beginning of God's work, and is the source of life to all who find her (8:30, 22, 35). The created order and human life seem to belong together.

---

[20] A. Peacocke, *Science and the Christian Experiment* (Oxford University Press, 1971), p. 133; *cf.* also his *Creation and the World of Science* (Clarendon, 1979) and *Theology for a Scientific Age* (SCM, 1990).

[21] Peacocke, *Science and the Christian Experiment*, p. 135.

[22] *E.g.* Matthew Fox, *Creation Spirituality* (HarperSanFrancisco, 1991).

It is fascinating how some contemporary cosmologists are reaching this sort of conclusion. Most reckon that our universe started very simply about 15,000 million years ago. It was an expanding ball of energy derived from what is often called the Big Bang. Some think that its ending will be a reversal of that expansion, with the universe collapsing back into itself – the Big Crunch. Happily, that is also a few thousand million years away. But the remarkable thing is that the universe that we experience now is a rich, varied, complicated place, and one of the most remarkable and complicated things about it is that you and I are here. In some of his writings John Polkinghorne tries a thought experiment. He wonders what would have happened if the force of gravity had been stronger than it is. Or what would have happened if electromagnetism were a bit weaker. The answer is that the expansion rate of the universe, and the chemicals that constitute it, would have been very different. Very small changes in what are called universal constants (gravity, electromagnetism, velocity of light, nuclear forces and so on – features of the make-up of our universe) would mean that we would not be here. For people like us, who can think and make relationships and fall in love, in other words for carbon-based organic life (which is what we are) to come into being, you would need the nuclear furnaces which we call the stars to burn for a very long time. These furnaces develop the heavier elements like carbon and oxygen from the very simple ones like hydrogen and helium; and it can be calculated that it takes several thousand million years for the nuclear and chemical processes needed to bring carbon-based life into being. This is what Polkinghorne says: 'We do not live at the centre of the universe, but neither do we live in just any old world. Instead we live in a universe whose constitution is precisely adjusted to the narrow limits which alone would make it capable of being our home.'[23]

Sir Bernard Lovell, former Director of Joddrell Bank, made the same point by asking why it is that the universe is expanding so near the critical rate to prevent its collapse. If the universe had begun to expand in the first few minutes after the explosion of its originally incredibly dense state by a rate minutely slower than it did, it would have collapsed back again relatively quickly. And if the expansion of the universe had been different only by a tiny fraction one way or the other from its actual rate, human existence would evidently have been impossible. 'But our measurements narrowly define one such universe, which had to be that particular universe if it was ever to be known and comprehended by an intelligent being.'[24]

[23] Polkinghorne, *op. cit.*
[24] Sir Bernard Lovell, F. W. Angel Memorial Lecture, 1977, quoted in T. F. Torrance, *The Ground and Grammar of Theology* (Christian Journals, Belfast, 1980), p. 3.

This is what some people call 'the anthropic principle', the idea that the way the universe is constituted is somehow tied up with the emergence of human life. We and the universe are profoundly bracketed together. In fact, science itself seems to be pointing to the importance of personal life. Once again we discover that it is not unreasonable – in fact it is extremely reasonable – to say that there is a personal being at the heart of all things. Proverbs points to the personal being we call God, and indicates that we know God as he makes himself known through his Wisdom.

Here is a statement of enormous importance, not only in reply to the defiant nihilism of Monod and the militant atheism of Dawkins, but also to those who are so captured by the contemporary theories of postmodernism that they have come to believe that (as the jargon goes) 'there are no metanarratives'. In other words, aspects of the postmodern culture (which is in large measure a very understandable reaction to some of the least satisfactory philosophical assumptions of the last two hundred years) suggest that there is nothing significant beyond the present, there is no meaning, there are no values, all is pastiche, nothing connects.

Not so, says Wisdom: everything connects, everything points back to a fundamental meaning and purpose in the mind of God. And more: that meaning and purpose are wonderfully personal. Christian theology much later developed this in terms of the doctrine of God the Holy Trinity. But Proverbs is giving us a pretty broad hint: at the back of all things are persons in relationship. That is what gives meaning and significance to our rationality, our morality, our love, our communication, our interconnectedness – in a word, our personhood.

Earlier we noted the importance to Wisdom of the whole of creation within which humanity has a special place. The faith underlying Proverbs says that human beings share this whole created order with all the rest of creation: it is all held in being by God's breath of life. But it also wants to avoid falling over into the materialism which simply puts human life on a par with all other life. There is in terms of our personal capacities something which sets us apart from the rest of the creation – namely that, unique among the animals, we humans have the gift and responsibility of being God's image: we can know God through his Wisdom. The ground of all things is Personal.

Fifthly, we underline a point we made briefly earlier: that the law of practical wisdom – how we live our lives in this world – is of a piece with the laws of the created universe. Just as the writer of Psalm 19 saw the laws of nature in the movement of the stars as inextricably linked to the moral law revealed by God to human beings, so Wisdom holds both these laws together in herself. There is something about the way we are created, and the moral universe in which we live our lives, which corresponds to the moral calling under which we are all invited to express God's image. The law of God for our behaviour corresponds with the way we are made and with the world in which he asks us to be moral agents.

There is a lot of confusion in the Christian church about moral issues, and behind that is confusion about Christian ways of making moral decisions. Some people operate with a view of morality which is really a matter of applying moral codes, which makes Christian ethics into nothing much more than keeping rules. Other people seem to abandon rules altogether, and try to decide what is good only on the basis of what will have the best outcome for the largest number of people. But if Wisdom holds together both the way we are made, and God's revelation of his will as to how we should behave, neither of these approaches is acceptable on its own.

It is insufficient to develop a morality in terms only of moral rules and codes, on the one hand, or in terms only of consequences (creating the greatest happiness for the greatest number), on the other. Rather, as Oliver O'Donovan puts it, discussing Christian freedom, the Holy Spirit 'forms and brings to expression the appropriate pattern of free response to objective reality';[25] a response which St Paul designates as love. 'Love is the overall shape of Christian ethics, the form of human participation in the created order.'[26] And love is itself ordered and shaped by the insights of the moral law, which describes both the created order and the character of God the creator, as these come to us in ways which require moral response.

Is this not the vision that is held out by Wisdom in Proverbs? As Tom Wright notes, Yahweh's wisdom means that when Yahweh created the world he did so wisely. But

... if 'wisdom' is thus the means by which Yahweh acts, and if human beings are then to become the means through which he acts, it is clear that wisdom is also precisely that which ... they need to be his agents, acting wisely under obedience to the creator and in authority over the world. And in obtaining wisdom, they will thereby become truly human.[27]

But here we need to note one other thing. There is something

---

[25] O. M. T. O'Donovan, *Resurrection and Moral Order* (IVP, 1986), p. 25.
[26] *Ibid.*
[27] N. T. Wright, *The New Testament and the People of God* (SPCK, 1992), pp. 264–265.

about Wisdom which is mysterious. She does not tell us all the answers. She invites us to consider certain situations she places before us in word pictures, and says to us: 'is this not how things are? If this is how the world is, how should you live now?' We are left with the responsibility of making moral choices, not simply obeying moral codes. The moral task is the process of being related to, not only guided by, God. As I put it elsewhere: 'Our lives tell the story of our relationship with God, a story we usually describe by the word "character". In contrast to [what he calls] "problem ethics", Dykstra speaks of Christian ethics as "visional" ethics, and writes:

> '"Decisions, choices and particular actions are not the first consideration in visional ethics. The foreground is occupied by questions concerning what we see and what it is that enables human beings to see more realistically. For visional ethics, action follows vision; and vision depends on character – a person thinking, reasoning, believing, feeling, willing and acting as a whole."'[28]

Finally, we can place this section of Proverbs 8 alongside a section from the apocryphal book of *Wisdom* (7:25–29), a book which surely influenced more than one of the writers of the New Testament. These sentences fill out from the pen of another poet many of these same themes, which come to their conclusion and completion in the man from Nazareth, the Christ of the New Testament gospel, though the feminine language and imagery they use remind us that God is beyond gender, and God's image is seen in male and female together.

> For she is a breath of the power of God,
>   and a pure emanation of the glory of the Almighty:
> therefore nothing defiled gains entrance into her.
> For she is a reflection of eternal light,
>   a spotless mirror of the working of God,
>   and an image of his goodness.
> Though she is but one, she can do all things,
>   and while remaining in herself, she renews all things;
> in every generation she passes into holy souls
>   and makes them friends of God, and prophets;
> for God loves nothing so much
>   as the man who lives with wisdom.

[28] D. Atkinson, 'Doctrine and Ethics', in Gordon Kuhrt (ed.), *Doctrine Matters* (Hodder and Stoughton, 1993), pp. 127–128, quoting Craig Dykstra, *Vision and Character* (Paulist Press, 1981), p. 36.

For she is more beautiful than the sun,
  and excels every constellation of the stars.
Compared with the light she is found to be superior.

(*Wisdom* 7:25–29, RSV)

So let us meet Wisdom, stately and lovely as she is (to use Horton's phrase), though she remains always a little inscrutable and unapproachable. We know her best because we know Christ who 'has become for us wisdom from God' (1 Cor. 1:30). He speaks her words with his own deeper meanings, but he also speaks his own Word which is his alone.

Part 2
Wisdom's instructors and Wisdom's detractors (1:1 – 9:18)

Many of the wisdom sayings in the first nine chapters of the book of Proverbs are addressed from a parent to a son. In Proverbs 1, both father and mother are mentioned as sharing in the instruction of the youth, an interesting contrast to other contemporary wisdom literature, in which only the fathers are mentioned. This serves to underline the importance of mothers in the Hebrew families. Although, as we said earlier, it is possible that some of these collections of sayings come from training manuals in the library of the leadership training-schools seeking to groom young men for future positions in the ruling court of Israel, their application is wider. Behind the language of the home, we may see the concerns of the sages of the wisdom schools. But behind both is the collected 'wisdom for life'. Perhaps we can think of the teachers casting themselves in the role of parents to their charges, and drawing on the sort of teaching that good parents might give their children.

It seems as though instructions given by parents and teachers in these chapters have in mind primarily the concerns of young adolescents, trying to discover who they are in the world, and how to behave. The parents are depicted as passing on wisdom which they learned in their younger days: 'When I was a boy in my father's house, still tender, and an only child of my mother, he taught me' (4:3–4). Clearly the home is depicted as one of the key institutions for the teaching of the young, and parents as well as teachers are trying to help the young people learn to discern the ways of wisdom.

This is not to suggest that the applications here are directed only at teenagers. The wisdom which is imparted in these chapters is wisdom for life at any age!

The pattern of teaching here is found elsewhere in the Old Testament: for example, in Deuteronomy 6:6–7. There God instructs his people: 'These commandments that I give you today are to be upon your hearts. Impress them on your children. Talk about them when you sit at home and when you walk along the road, when you lie down and when you get up.' Parts of the New Testament also point to the home as the place of education: 'I have been reminded of your sincere faith, which first lived in your grandmother Lois and in your mother Eunice and, I am persuaded, now lives in you also . . . how from infancy you have known the holy Scriptures' (2 Tim. 1:5; 3:15).

Ten fatherly talks

In Proverbs 1 – 9 there are ten separate sections of 'fatherly talks'. Whybray calls them the 'Ten Discourses' or 'Ten Instructions', and compares them with the Egyptian school instruction books which have similar form and content.[1] These fatherly talks, or discourses, practically all follow a similar pattern. Thus (a) there is an introductory address, 'My son', or something similar, followed by (b) an instruction to hear, receive or be attentive. Then (c) the virtue of Wisdom in one or another of her forms is extolled, and the son is told to clothe himself with it. (d) The main theme of each discourse then follows, usually with an exhortation or a prohibition or a command. (e) Finally, the talk ends with a reflection on either the happy state of the righteous or the fate of the wicked or the fool. We can illustrate this by briefly outlining the sections in question.

Talks about evil company (1:8–19)

(a) My son (8).
(b) Listen to instruction, do not forsake teaching (8).
(c) Wisdom is like a garland (9).
(d) Beware of evil company (10–15).
(e) In fact evil people waylay only themselves (16–19).

This section, which we will have occasion to look at in more detail in a few moments, is a warning against getting mixed up in the wrong company, which can easily lead to temptations to organized robbery and even murder. Perhaps Jerusalem had a criminal underclass. There are references in some of the earlier prophets (Amos, Hosea, Micah) to organized, even legalized, oppression of the poor by the rich. The wise teacher recognizes that the temptations for the youth will be strong, but also that, unresisted, they will be disastrous.

---

[1] Cf. Whybray, *Proverbs*, and *Wisdom in Proverbs*.

Talks about avoiding wicked men and the lure of the adulteress (2:1–22)

(a) My son (1).
(b) Accept, store up, turn your ear, apply your heart, call out for insight, cry aloud for understanding, look, search (1–5).
(c) Wisdom is a treasure (4) from God (6); her riches shield, guard and protect (7–12).
(d) By understanding the right path (9), you will be saved from wicked men (12) and from the adulteress (16–19).
(e) The upright will live, but the wicked will be cut off (21–22).

This is another paragraph to which we shall return for more detailed discussion. There are people in the city who can lead the young man astray. Some are men *whose words are perverse*; some are women who seduce with flattering words. The wise teacher warns the young man to avoid them.

The following two 'instruction' sections in Proverbs 3 serve as a central focus for most of Wisdom's 'instructions' in these chapters. The section 3:1–12 is essentially a reflection on what it means to love God; in 3:21–35 the interest is in love towards our neighbour. In between (3:13–20) is one of the portraits of Wisdom, the wisdom of Yahweh, which we looked at in our previous chapter. The shape of Proverbs 3, therefore, indicates the underlying philosophy of much of the whole book. Yahweh is at the centre of things, and his ways are made known through Wisdom. The implications of living in Wisdom's way are that we will be drawn first to love God, and then that that love will show itself towards our neighbours.

We will first notice the way in which both these sections fit into a didactic pattern similar to all the other 'instruction' sections, and then we will comment on both sections together.

Talks about duty to God (3:1–12)

(a) My son (1).
(b) Do not forget (1).
(c) Love and faithfulness are to be bound around your neck, and written on the tablet of your heart (3–4).
(d) A right attitude to God is trust, acknowledgment, fear. He is to be honoured with our wealth, and respected in his discipline (9–12).
(e) For the godly, there is satisfaction (10) on the one hand, and loving discipline (11) on the other.

Talks about duty to the neighbour (3:21–35)

(a) My son (21).
(b) Preserve sound judgment (21).
(c) Wisdom is an adornment for the neck (22).
(d) The way of wisdom will bring safety (23), security (24) and confidence in God (26), which are to be reflected in care for the neighbour (27–31).
(e) The perverse man is detested by God, the wicked are cursed; but the wise inherit honour (32–35).

As we said above, both these sections seem to summarize most of the rest of the 'instruction' sections of Proverbs 1 – 9. It will be useful at this point to pause and pick out the main themes.

Proverbs 3:1–12

Love to God is essentially reactive. *Love and faithfulness* (3) are central words in the covenant relationship between Yahweh and his people. They prompt *trust* (5), *fear* (= reverent obedience) (7), responsible stewardship of God's gifts (9–10), and a willingness to learn through *discipline* (11–12).

The similarity of Proverbs 3:1–4 to Deuteronomy 6:1–15 has often been noted. There Yahweh is the teacher, and Israel is the 'son' (*cf.* Pr. 3:1). There Israel is called on to be obedient, and will be rewarded with long life and prosperity (*cf.* Pr. 3:2). God's commands are to be upon their hearts, impressed on their children, talked about at home, tied as symbols on their hands and bound on their foreheads (Dt. 6:6–9; *cf.* Pr. 3:3). The Deuteronomy passage is all about loving God with heart and soul and strength. The language of Proverbs 3:1–12 is very similar. In both Proverbs and Deuteronomy, the education of the young people begins with an acknowledgment of Yahweh's covenanted faithfulness and the call to *acknowledge* him *in all your ways* (Pr. 3:6).

The benefits of trusting the LORD are, first, *favour and a good name in the sight of God and man* (4); in other words, a good reputation with everyone; the respect and benefits which flow from godliness. Secondly, *he will make your paths straight* (6), a metaphor derived from road-building (as in Is. 40:3), which suggests that *trust in the LORD* will smooth out all a person's rough paths. We shall need to come back to this thought later in our study, but notice now that this is the language of faith, not necessarily of constant experience. There are plenty of examples later in Proverbs of life's way which is not very smooth. The point here is that the believer is being encouraged to trust in the LORD even when things are unclear, and to *lean not on your own understanding* even when we think we know best. For the God who holds the future can see further than we can, and his covenanted love is promised as a deeper security than anything our dimmer understanding can comprehend or our straining eyes can glimpse.

To *trust in the* LORD, to *acknowledge him*, to *fear the* LORD *and shun evil*, also brings *health to your body and nourishment to your bones. Body* and *bones* refer to our whole selves, and the picture here is of health which touches every part of the person. Health in the Bible is a holistic word: to be whole is to be in the right with God at all levels of our being. This is not to say that trust in the LORD will ensure permanent physical health; once again there is plenty in Proverbs which talks about sickness and depression. It is to say that spiritual, emotional and bodily well-being are all bound up together: we human beings are psychosomatic-spiritual unities. It is also to say that walking in God's way is to walk the way of wholeness for the whole of our being.

Verses 9–10 take further the theme of honouring God and the prosperity which results from doing so. At first sight this seems to promote a rather dubious motive: honour God so that you will be made rich! But once again we must stand back from this and notice the link between this chapter and Deuteronomy, this time chapter 26. There the people of God are told to offer to God the firstfruits of what their land produces (Dt. 26:2, 10). There the offering back to God of what was his gift was a liturgical way of recognizing God's gift of the promised land – and therefore that the worshipper was a part of that gift. To offer the firstfruits to God was a way of celebrating God's deliverance and God's provision – and a means by which each person could appreciate that he or she was part of that story. So here in Proverbs, the honouring of God *with our wealth* is not a shady piece of manipulation to ensure that God makes you richer still. It is first of all a response to God's generosity – the land and all its wealth belongs to God and I am called to be his steward – and a statement of gratitude that I am included in God's gracious deliverance and provision. The sense is that captured in King David's prayer at a different time and in a different place:

> Praise be to you, O LORD,
> God of our father Israel,
> from everlasting to everlasting.
> Yours, O LORD, is the greatness and the power
> and the glory and the majesty and the splendour,
> for everything in heaven and earth is yours . . .
> Wealth and honour come from you . . .

Everything comes from you, and we have given you only what comes from your hand.[2]

But then we note that the prosperity envisaged is of a particular sort: it is *barns* and *vats*, bread and wine – the staple food which makes life possible and which can be shared with the poor and needy (*cf.* 3:27). As Matthew Henry amusingly comments:

He does not say thy bags, but thy barns, not thy wardrobe replenished, but thy presses; God shall bless thee with an increase of that which is for use, not for show or ornament; for spending and laying out, not for hoarding and laying up. They that do good with what they have shall have more to do good with.

Or as Hubbard puts it, 'Prosperity, gratitude and charity are an indivisible triad of experiences in biblical thought.'

The final two verses of this first section move us from love to discipline. However well intentioned the believer may be to walk in the LORD's way, there will be failure. It is part of the LORD's love to exercise that measure of discipline which brings a wayward person back on to the path. Here is an early acknowledgment that the promised prosperity referred to in previous verses does not always translate into a pain-free life. The corrective love of God, as Hebrews 12:5–7 also says, quoting these verses, can sometimes mean 'hardship and discipline'. Now here again we can make logical connections and find ourselves talking nonsense. Just as we cannot read the earlier verses to mean that a life of faith will be trouble-free, so we may not read these verses to equate all life's difficulties with God's correction, as though all suffering came from sin. The New Testament many times makes clear that this is too easy an equation (*cf.* Jn. 9:2–3). However, it is salutary to reflect on how far our culture and our church have moved from the convictions of earlier generations, which sought to interpret the sufferings of life as part of the discipline of God, and to learn from our struggles something of the character of Christ.

Referring to this text, the service for the Visitation of the Sick in the Anglican *Book of Common Prayer* includes these statements:

These words, good brother or sister, are written in holy Scripture for our comfort and instruction; that we should patiently, and with thanksgiving, bear our heavenly Father's correction, whensoever by any manner of adversity it shall please his gracious

---

[2] 1 Ch. 29:10–14.

goodness to visit us. And there should be no greater comfort to Christian persons, than to be made like unto Christ, by suffering patiently adversities, troubles and sicknesses. For he himself went not up to joy, but first he suffered pain; he entered not into his glory before he was crucified.

Proverbs 3:1–12, then, focuses our attention on love to God, which is expressed in keeping his commands (3), trusting his leading (5–8), honouring him with gratitude for all our possessions (9–10), and accepting his correction (11–12).

After the next paragraph (3:13–20), which we discussed earlier, Wisdom now continues her teaching.

Proverbs 3:21–35

This section we have described as 'duty to the neighbour'. It is made up of different bits and pieces of advice. Verse 21 is a sort of introduction, reminding the learner of the prudence involved in preserving *sound judgment*. Verses 22–26 bring the reader's mind back to the earlier theme of confidence in Yahweh. His wisdom will give *life* (22) and safety (23–24). There is no need for sudden panic (25), because Yahweh *will be your confidence* (26). Then verses 27–35 deal with different aspects of social behaviour which give cash value in human relationships to the way of Wisdom. First of all, Wisdom emphasizes the importance of honesty and promptness in repaying loans (27–28). In more general terms, we can understand verse 27 as setting out the central principle of generosity: *Do not withhold good from those who deserve it, when it is in your power to act.* Then Wisdom urges her pupil to avoid premeditated conspiracy to harm someone else (29). It is important to refuse to pick a quarrel (30),[3] and to recognize that crime does not pay (31). In summary, these verses are about generosity. The security and protection which come from Yahweh (21–26) put us under an obligation to be generous to the disadvantaged (to provide for their needs) and to the neighbourhood (to be a peacemaker).

The closing verses (33–35) provide a sort of epilogue to the whole chapter, contrasting wisdom and folly, scorn and grace, God's blessing and God's curse. Verse 34 is quoted in the New Testament, where James is urging his readers to submit to God, and to be peacemakers in the community. What gets in the way of both is pride before God and self-centred motives in dealing with others. 'God opposes the proud but gives grace to the humble' (Jas. 4:6). This same verse is quoted in the first letter of Peter (5:6), in the context of

---

[3] *Cf.* Whybray, *Proverbs*, comment on verse 30.

an appeal for humility. The fact that the same verse is used in these different New Testament letters may suggest that it was familiar as part of an early Christian teaching document or perhaps liturgy. The theme is nowhere illustrated more fully and more wonderfully than in the Song of Mary (Lk. 1:46–55):

> My soul glorifies the Lord
>   and my spirit rejoices in God my Saviour,
> for he has been mindful
>   of the humble state of his servant.
> From now on all generations will call me blessed,
>   for the Mighty One has done great things for me –
> holy is his name.
> His mercy extends to those who fear him,
>   from generation to generation.
> He has performed mighty deeds with his arm;
>   he has scattered those who are proud in their inmost thoughts.
> He has brought down rulers from their thrones
>   but has lifted up the humble.
> He has filled the hungry with good things
>   but has sent the rich away empty.
> He has helped his servant Israel,
>   remembering to be merciful
> to Abraham and his descendants for ever,
>   even as he said to our fathers.

We can now move on in our study of Proverbs 1 – 9, to notice that the pattern of these 'instruction' sections in Proverbs 1 – 3 is also followed in later chapters. In chapter 4, for instance, there are three sections: about Wisdom herself, about evil company, and about vigilance.

Talks about Wisdom herself (4:1–9)

(a) My sons (1).
(b) Listen, pay attention, do not forsake teaching (1–2).
(c) Wisdom herself garlands your head (9).
(d) Get wisdom, as I your father did (3–7).
(e) When wisdom is esteemed, you will be exalted (8).

This rich little paragraph revolves around the central point that in the education process, we learn most of all from those around us, especially those in our families. This father (1) learned from his father and mother (3), and is passing the wisdom on to his sons (1). All of us, for good or ill, are inevitably shaped to some degree by who our parents were; and we inevitably shape the next generation.

What for some become 'cycles of deprivation'[4] can for others thankfully be 'cycles of affirmation'.[5] There is a 'chain of tradition linking the wisdom of the generations', as Hubbard puts it. He goes on: 'Breaking the bad cycles and continuing the good ones are what wise parenting entails.'[6] This teacher (1) is fortunate that he can look back to his own parents with gratitude that their wisdom has brought him a *crown of splendour* (9).

More talks about evil company (4:10–19)

(a) My son (10).
(b) Listen, accept what I say (10).
(c) Guard wisdom, she is your life (13).
(d) Avoid the way of evil men (14–17).
(e) The path of the righteous is light, that of the wicked is deep darkness (18–19).

The father's instruction continues now with some practical admonitions. He has led his pupils up *straight paths* (11), not the *path of the wicked* (14). *The path of the righteous is like* the light *of dawn* (18). So the student must be careful where he walks (*cf.* 26). Many of the verbs are to do with leading, walking, running and stumbling. The *path*, then, is a metaphor for a particular way of living. It depicts a style of behaviour, an attitude to life, a character. The wise teacher encourages his pupils to develop the style, attitude and character that will lead to *life* (13). Because of this, it is important to avoid the stumbling-blocks on the way.

The major stumbling-block referred to in this paragraph is *the way of evil men* (14). We will look in more detail shortly at the lure of the gangs of violence referred to in chapter 1. But they feature here also in verses 14–17. Such people *cannot sleep till they do evil . . . till they make someone fall* (16). *Violence* is food and drink to them (17). Avoid them.

Talks about vigilance (4:20–27)

(a) My son (20).
(b) Pay attention, listen closely (20).
(c) The words of wisdom are to be kept in your heart; they are life and health (21–22).

[4] A reference to a phrase used by Sir Keith Joseph in a speech in 1972, when he was Secretary of State for Social Services.
[5] The title of a marvellous book by Christian psychiatrist Jack Dominian (Darton, Longman and Todd, 1975).
[6] Hubbard, pp. 80–81.

(d) Be on guard (23) – in what you are (23), in what you say (24), in what you see (25), and in where you go (26–27).
(e) Then the way of the vigilant will be firm ground (26).

The father's instructions here remind the pupils of yet another stumbling-block on the path to life against which they are to be on their guard and be vigilant: namely, dishonest talk. To be caught up into the life of the group, especially when it is a gang bent on violence, can. so very easily prevent us from standing back and making an honest assessment of our situation. We justify attitudes and actions to ourselves on the ground that 'others do it, too'. Or we simply fail to notice when we are caught up in collusion with what is devious. The father's word here is 'Be vigilant'; dishonesty and deviousness cause people to leave the right path.

The next three 'instruction' sections (5:1–23; 6:20–35; 7:1–27) also follow the same pattern that we have seen up until now. They are all concerned about the 'loose woman', the 'adulteress', whose role in Proverbs 1 – 9 we will discuss in much more detail in a short while.

Finally, we turn to Proverbs chapter 6:1–19.

General talks, warning against folly (6:1–19)

This little section, though still addressed to *My son* (1), does not follow the same structure exactly. But its themes fit with the rest:

The virtue of prudence (1–5).
The folly of laziness (6–11).
The evil of deceitfulness (12–15).
The things the LORD hates: pride, lies, murder, deviousness, dissension (16–19).

There is first of all a warning here not to make a rash commitment which we may find ourselves in the event unable to keep. We must try to disengage ourselves, even if it means eating humble pie (1–5). This is a good example of the practical and prudential emphasis that we find throughout Proverbs. The heart of this section is not the suggestion that you should not make commitments, but rather the need for willingness to apologize, to admit a mistake, and to disentangle yourself from an inappropriate and rash pledge. This rather goes against a culture which refuses ever to admit a mistake, but is a word of practical prudence needed to free up relationships.

The second few verses (6–11) are a vivid warning against laziness, and a call to learn diligence even from the *ant*. The danger that the pupil will become a *sluggard* is a theme we pick up again shortly.

Verses 12–15 comment on the eventual disaster which will befall those who plot evil ways. The young people need to be warned against such 'scoundrels and villains'.

Finally, verses 16–19 list *six* or *seven* things which *the LORD hates*. As elsewhere in Proverbs, the numerical pattern helps the reader to remember what is being said, and perhaps focuses the development of the pattern towards its concluding saying. The LORD hates *haughty eyes, a lying tongue*, killing of *innocent* human beings, *wicked schemes* (perhaps this includes the miscarriage of justice through the falsification of evidence against the innocent), and, perhaps especially, the stirring up of *dissension* within the community. Hubbard comments on this paragraph that the legal systems 'in which someone has to win big and another lose lavishly whenever claims are made cannot be right'.[7] There are social patterns which promote discord in communities. These are not the ways of Wisdom: the LORD hates such things.

Wisdom's detractors

Apart perhaps from chapter 6, all the other 'instruction' paragraphs in these chapters give much positive teaching, providing us with a portrait of Wisdom which includes creativity, justice, integrity and vitality. Chapter 3 in particular mostly offers a very positive and life-giving set of instructions. But there are some more negative sections in these early chapters of Proverbs, in which the teachers are warning their pupils, and the parents are warning their teenage sons, about the sorts of things which get in the way of wisdom. It will be helpful now to review some of these sections once more, to discuss Wisdom's detractors more fully. These are not so very far from the struggles many parents have in knowing how to respond to adolescent concerns now, as young people work at the emotional and personal tasks of adolescence which Erikson has most helpfully summarized as the quest for a sense of 'identity'.[8] If that task is not undertaken successfully, perhaps because of inadequate management of earlier life crises in the processes of infantile development, the adolescent's life may be marked by what Erikson calls 'role confusion'. 'Who am I? And where do I belong?' We will pick out four particular themes from these chapters of Proverbs: gang violence, sexual experimentation, laziness, and mocking rejection of parental values. Let us see how these parental talks handle these themes.

---

[7] *Ibid.*, p. 103.
[8] *Cf.* Erik Erikson, 'The Eight Ages of Man', in *Childhood and Society* (Triad/Granada, 1977), pp. 222ff.

Gang violence (1:10–19)

The situation envisaged is pictured graphically here. The young man is warned against the likelihood of being enticed (10) into violent ways (11–12). The gang holds out hopes of quick pickings (13), and the promise of shared rewards (14). But Wisdom warns them (15) that such wickedness (16) will lead only to disaster (18–19).

> *My son, if sinners entice you,*
>   *do not give in to them.*
> [11]*If they say, 'Come along with us;*
>   *let's lie in wait for someone's blood,*
>   *let's waylay some harmless soul;*
> [12]*let's swallow them alive, like the grave,*
>   *and whole, like those who go down to the pit;*
> [13]*we will get all sorts of valuable things*
>   *and fill our houses with plunder;*
> [14]*throw in your lot with us,*
>   *and we will share a common purse' –*
> [15]*my son, do not go along with them,*
>   *do not set foot on their paths;*
> [16]*for their feet rush into sin,*
>   *they are swift to shed blood.*
> [17]*How useless to spread a net*
>   *in full view of all the birds!*
> [18]*These men lie in wait for their own blood;*
>   *they waylay only themselves!*
> [19]*Such is the end of all who go after ill-gotten gain;*
>   *it takes away the lives of those who get it.*

The wise parents in this paragraph are seeking to warn their son about the company he keeps, urging him not to go with the enticements of the gang. There is always something attractive about simply going with the crowd. Perhaps in the setting in Israel, we are intended to understand this in the middle of city life. Wisdom, after all, calls in the noisy streets (1:20). The young men have left their villages and are seeking to make a living in Jerusalem, where they will rub shoulders with those who do not acknowledge Israel's God. They are *sinners* (10), some of whom are known for terrorism, hijacking, looting, even murder. The godly parents urge their son not to go along with them, for they can see where it will all end. It will not in fact yield *all sorts of valuable things* (13); it is *their own blood* that will be forfeit, their own selves who are waylaid (18). The greed of verse 12 in fact only diminishes the lives of the greedy. Can the teenager understand the longer-term picture? These short-term enticements to go with the gang, to take part in violence and intimidation of others, to grab and plunder, will not in fact bring the sense of belonging, happiness and identity that is sought; it will not remove the confusion in the adolescent mind. It will only reinforce destructive and dehumanizing attitudes, they seem to say – and the person who will get most hurt will be you. Here are caring and compassionate parents urging their youth to avoid the dangers of the gang.

As human beings made in the image of God the Holy Trinity, we are persons in networks of relationships with other persons. The quality of the relationships we make with others will affect others' lives; the quality of the relationships they make with us will affect our own. Furthermore, the general principle emphasized here is that the persons we are is to a large extent determined by the company we keep.

Not only in parenting adolescents, but in all our contexts of human interrelationships, the wisdom of this paragraph helps us place the attractiveness of the moment in the context of the long-term picture, and the likely outcomes of particular ways of behaving. What story do we want our lives to tell? Where do these particular actions in the present fit into that larger story? When we look back on the stories of our lives, how will we then see this or that particular action which at the time seemed so attractive, but in the long term has been so destructive? These parental warnings about avoiding the gangs are not only prudent cautions about the present. They are also part of the process by which characters are formed and the stories of our lives are written, which – from the perspective of the future – will be seen to have been life-giving rather than the way of death.

Sexual promiscuity

Another serious concern of these parents is that their youth will be lured away from the possibilities of real sexual fulfilment by the enticements of promiscuity. Several times these chapters offer warnings against *the adulteress*. In contrast to the life-giving character of Wisdom, this adulterous woman can do only harm. She appears first in 2:16–19.

Proverbs 2:16–19

The *adulteress*, or *wayward wife* (16) who has abandoned her spouse (17), tries to seduce the young man (16), but the path to her door is the way of *death* (18–22). At one level, this paragraph is about sexual temptation and the warnings which the young do well to heed. At another, this figure stands for the opposite of Wisdom: another woman is seeking attention, but her ways are not life-giving, and her rewards are only destructive.

> *It will save you also from the adulteress,*
>   *from the wayward wife with her seductive words,*
> [17]*who has left the partner of her youth*
>   *and ignored the covenant she made before God.*
> [18]*For her house leads down to death*
>   *and her paths to the spirits of the dead.*
> [19]*None who go to her return*
>   *or attain the paths of life.*

Here the adulteress is depicted as a married woman who has left her husband, *and ignored the* marriage *covenant she made before God.* She has put herself outside the community of God's people, and the voice of Wisdom is heard warning the young man against her alluring ways. She is able to seduce the young with her words, but the path of adultery in fact leads in the opposite direction from the life-giving way pointed out by Wisdom. To go with the loose woman is to walk off the path of life.

Christopher Wright has made it clear that there is perhaps more in the RSV's phrase 'loose woman' (NIV *adulteress*) than we might immediately appreciate. There has been much discussion of the meaning of the word translated 'loose' – whether it means 'foreign' or 'outside the family'. Wright argues that by her repudiation of her own marriage vows, she has put herself 'outside' her own family. In the Old Testament, family loyalties were intended to reflect the loyalty of the covenant God to his people, and theirs to him. The marriage covenant and the covenant with Yahweh were analogies of each other. This makes even more significant the use of the word *covenant* in 2:17: by forsaking the *partner* of her youth, the loose woman forgets the covenant of her God. By betraying her covenant of marriage, this woman looses herself from the covenant community and turns her back on the covenant of God. No wonder the end of her road is death, which is separation from the life-giving relationship with God. This is why the warning to the young man is emphasized so strongly.

Inheriting the land, and being cut off from the land, are features of God's covenant people and their loyalty to him or their disobedience. To get entangled with a woman who has loosed herself from the covenant obligations of the people of God is to jeopardize one's own place within the covenant, and to risk being cut off from all that sustains life in the land which belongs to God's people. Such a man is cut off from his family, and thereby from the life of the family of God. That is why this is so serious.

The loose woman comes back again in chapter 5, where the whole chapter sets up the contrast between the satisfying sexual fulfilment of a faithful covenanted relationship, and the strength-sapping, disease-ridden way of adultery. As earlier, this is one of the 'instruction' sections and follows the familiar pattern.

Proverbs 5:1–23

(a) My son (1).
(b) Pay attention, listen well (1).
(c) Wisdom is discretion (2).
(d) Do not go near the temptations and dangers of the loose woman (3–20).
(e) A man's ways are in full view of the LORD (21); the wicked is ensnared in his evil deeds (22–23).

The loose woman is the focus of interest in the opening section of this chapter (1–8), which then moves into a reflection on the fate which the adulteress may expect from the *assembly* (that is, the local community) (9–14). The lovely section of verses from 5:15 to 19, extolling the delight of marital faithfulness, concludes (20) with another exhortation to avoid the *adulteress*, and with a general reflection on the judgment and providence of God (21–23).

The verses at the heart of this chapter celebrate the joy of sexual fidelity. The Bible does not hide its delight at God's purpose for human sexuality. The erotic delight of sexual embrace is expressed in the language of refreshment and blessing. *Love* in verse 19 means love-making. Let the young man find joy in making love to the wife of his youth. But these passions are not to be shared with strangers. In fact the teacher suggests that in comparison with the rich fulfilment of appropriate sexual expression in a relationship of love and faithfulness, to imagine that the adulteress has anything to offer is sheer stupidity.

We should notice Wisdom's progress in this paragraph from exclusivity (*Let them be yours alone*, 17), to joy (18), to the commonsense response ('Why look elsewhere?', 20), to divine judgment (*a man's ways are in full view of the* LORD, 21). This all illustrates what we may call the law of moral providence (22–23).

Around this lovely little paragraph (15–19), Wisdom again warns about the adulteress. Her *lips . . . drip honey, and her speech is smoother than oil,* but it is all *as bitter as gall* (3–4). The language of the rest of Wisdom's instructions is very strong: *crooked, cruel, groan, the brink of utter ruin* (6–14). She ends with the question, *Why be captivated, my son, by an adulteress? Why embrace the bosom of another man's wife?*

The second half of chapter 6 picks up the same theme again, and follows the pattern of 'instruction'.

Proverbs 6:20–35

(a) My son (20).
(b) Keep commands, do not forsake teaching (20).
(c) Wisdom's teaching is to be bound on your heart and fastened around your neck (21).
(d) Various commandments to avoid the allure of the prostitute (23–26).
(e) Sexual immorality leads to suffering, dishonour, jealousy, revenge (27–35).

Verses 20–25 contain instructions from the teacher to the student: the *father's commands* and *mother's teaching* (20) will *guide, watch* and instruct (22–23). If you follow them you will be kept *from the immoral woman* (24): *do not lust* after her (25). Then follows a more general comment on the dangers of promiscuity (26–29), and the chapter concludes with a comparison between the adulterer and someone who steals food because he is hungry (30–35). Though the petty thief may escape with only a fine (31), even though that may be heavy (31), the adulterer can never escape a jealous *husband's fury* (34), and has to live with disgrace all his life (33). By contrast with the light of Wisdom's lamp, illuminating the way of life (23), the smooth-talking immoral woman *preys upon your very life* (26).

The writer now uses vivid metaphors to drive the point home. *Can a man scoop fire into his lap without his clothes being burned? Can a man walk on hot coals without his feet being scorched?* (27–28). Of course not! *So is he who sleeps with another man's wife; no-one who touches her will go unpunished.* To give way to lust like this means that you will get burned.

It does not need Aids and other sexually transmitted diseases to remind us of the destructiveness of promiscuity. Sex without commitment is actually to live a lie.

It is by following the words and ways of Wisdom that the young man will be kept on the path of life. The 'instruction' section of chapter 7 fills out the theme once more.

Proverbs 7:1–27

(a) My son (1).
(b) Keep my words and store my commands (1).
(c) Wisdom's words are to be bound on your fingers and written on the tablet of your heart (3).

(d) Do not stray into the paths of the temptress (25); she has many seductive ways (6–23).

(e) Those who follow the immoral woman become her victims; her path leads to the chambers of death (27).

The writer begins again by urging the young man to heed Wisdom's words (1–4); by so doing the ways of the adulteress can be avoided (5). Then we are offered a rich picture of the loose woman's wiles (6–23), observed from a neighbouring *window* (6). Her dress (10), style (11) and approach (13) are all described, along with the enticements she has to offer (14–20). The young man is led *astray* (21–23). He goes blindly into danger like the *ox* (22) or the *bird* (23); danger approaches him like 'fetters coming to the chastisement of a fool' as Toy translates the *deer stepping into a noose* of 22), or as an *arrow* piercing the entrails (23). He does not know that *it will cost him his life* (23). The chapter closes (24–27) by picking up the thought of verse 5, and emphasizes the warnings.

For the young man in the big city, the enticements of sexual exploration are sometimes very strong. The prostitutes can be very persuasive. Short-term sexual recreation seems very attractive. But from Wisdom's perspective, it is *like a deer stepping into a noose* or a *bird darting into a snare*. Wisdom wants the young man to be protected from such destructiveness, disillusionment and disappointment. Wisdom wants the young man to *live* (2).

Once again, the parents are seeking to help the young persons to understand the actions of the present in the light of the larger story of their lives, and what they want that story to tell when they eventually look back on the present. It is the preciousness of sexual intimacy in its appropriate covenant context which makes it necessary to say no to inappropriate intimacy in other contexts. These parents are not afraid to make the boundaries clear. But their teaching is not only prohibition: it draws on personal experiences to illustrate why the prohibitions make sense. Chapter 7 in particular paints a vivid picture of young people congregating on the street corner (7). The teacher has stood in his window at evening light, and watched what happens. There is one young man who made the choice to follow the harlot's invitation. He is trapped by her lustful seductions, which are made worse by the fact that she is apparently a religious person, who wishes to use the rituals of peace offerings (obviously with plenty of food in the house!), and making vows, while at the same time satisfying her sexual needs.

In the Christian church today, there are young people who are still wanting to keep to the traditional ethic of sexual relationships within marriage. But many of them are not really sure why they do. One way towards suggesting an answer is to pick up the importance attached to covenanted commitment which these sections of Proverbs indicate. To have a full sexual relationship with somebody is to give physical expression to what is meant to be a covenanted relationship – that is, stable, faithful, permanent. To say physically, 'I am giving myself to you', while emotionally and spiritually holding back from covenanted commitment is in fact to live a lie – a split in the personality which is ultimately stressful and destructive. This is the sort of argument used by St Paul in 1 Corinthians 6 where he chides his readers for thinking that they can enjoy a physical sexual relationship with a prostitute without its having any significance for their emotional and spiritual health. Not so, he says. The sexual relationship is itself a commitment. It is ultimately disastrous for your body to be saying something that your heart does not mean. It is better to *Say to Wisdom, 'You are my sister'*, to *call* her *understanding your kinsman* (7:4) and to learn from her the covenanted commitment that can lead to joy (5:18).

Laziness

There is a further temptation ready to deflect the adolescent youth from the paths of Wisdom: laziness. As the cartoon put it: 'Why should anyone work, when he has the health and strength to stay in bed?' It is so tempting to stay in bed, especially when you would rather not face the day. It is easier to postpone decisions and actions until another time. There is too much going on in the adolescent's mind to cope with: better to opt out and let time pass. It might be easier when we wake up.

Wisdom knows all about such patterns of behaviour. But the truth is that if you give way to such laziness, that too will endanger your livelihood, or even your life. We return to the picture drawn in the earlier part of chapter 6. Verses 6–11 provide an example of the sort of wisdom writing which uses the animal world to give lessons in good behaviour. The same device is used later in chapter 30. Here analogies are drawn with the ant. The consequences of laziness are vividly pointed up by comparison with the ant who manages, without being told (7), to make appropriate provision for the future (8). In contrast to such 'wisdom', the *sluggard* (6, 9) who stays in bed too long (9–10) will find that his laziness results in *poverty* (11).

> *Go to the ant, you sluggard;*
> *consider its ways and be wise!*
> *⁷It has no commander,*
> *no overseer or ruler,*
> *⁸yet it stores its provisions in summer*
> *and gathers its food at harvest.*

> [9]*How long will you lie there, you sluggard?*
>   *When will you get up from your sleep?*
> [10]*A little sleep, a little slumber,*
>   *a little folding of the hands to rest –*
> [11]*and poverty will come on you like a bandit*
>   *and scarcity like an armed man.*

Laziness is an abandonment of responsibility – a failure, often, of love. If you stay in bed when you should be working, do not be surprised if you run out of money, or the food stocks run down (11).

With heavy irony, the writer draws a contrast between this large, gawky, adolescent lazybones, and the small, insignificant, industrious ant. The ant does not have a leader – not like the youth, who perhaps is being trained up to be a member of the king's court. But the ant thinks ahead, and *stores its provisions in the summer* and *at harvest* time to make sure there is enough to last through the year. The youths are going to have to overcome their laziness if they are to survive, take their own responsibilities, and not be a drain on everyone else.

Rejection of parental values

Adolescence is also a time when young people have major decisions to make about their own moral character.[9] Early on in life, most of us start our moral development with what we might call a 'prudential' morality. We learn right from wrong by discovering that if we overstep the mark, we will get hurt – by our parents' displeasure, if not by their physical discipline. Later on, through friends, school and peer pressures, we develop what we may call an 'authoritarian' morality. Our understanding of right and wrong derives from some authority which we respect and obey – the authority of our parents, perhaps, or our teachers, our friends or our heroes. But adolescence is a time when we are called on to develop a more 'personal' morality. We have to take responsibility for deciding which of these authorities we will accept, which we will still go along with, and which we can no longer respect. And for some of us adolescence is a time for overthrowing all our given authorities, and trying to find our own. That is partly why we are open to being enticed by the gang, or lured by the prostitute. But Wisdom cautions against such a wholesale overthrow of received values. Wisdom certainly wants the young person to take responsibility for his or her own choices; it is important that morality becomes 'personal'. But that does not mean throwing over everything from the past. That is the way of cynicism

[9] See J. Dominian, *Authority* (Darton, Longman and Todd, 1976), for a good discussion.

and pride. It is also very hurtful and destructive.

The mocker, then, features in Wisdom's list of detractors. The mocker does not like being corrected and pointed in the way of wisdom.

There is a little paragraph in chapter 9 which refers to the sort of responses that might be expected by someone who tries to give instruction to a *mocker* or 'scoffer'. In contrast to the wise person who responds to rebuke with *love* (8), and to instruction by growth in wisdom (9), the mocker responds to correction with *insult* (7), and to rebuke with hatred (8).

> *Whoever corrects a mocker invites insult;*
> *whoever rebukes a wicked man incurs abuse.*
> *[8]Do not rebuke a mocker or he will hate you;*
> *rebuke a wise man and he will love you.*
> *[9]Instruct a wise man and he will be wiser still;*
> *teach a righteous man and he will add to his learning.*

The mocker features in later chapters also (13:1; 15:12). By his mocking rejection of his teacher's words, he displays the pride (21:24) which just makes trouble. 'Drive out the mocker, and out goes strife; quarrels and insults are ended' (22:10). People detest them (24:9). They stir up whole communities (29:8). Wisdom warns the young man not to fall into mocking ways.

Problem pupils

There are a number of characters depicted throughout Proverbs who seem unable or unwilling to learn Wisdom's ways. This is an appropriate point at which to pause and remind ourselves of some of them: the simple, the fool and the scoffer. Kidner's commentary helpfully draws out some of the notable features of each.

Proverbs addresses itself throughout this section to young men – and Kidner follows this in his references to 'he', 'him' – but we must not overlook the extent to which we all find ourselves figuring in the picture, old as well as young, women as well as men.

The *simple* in Proverbs are people who just do not think. Kidner describes such a person as 'easily led, gullible, silly. Mentally, he is naïve ("the simple believes everything, but the prudent looks where he is going", 14:15; *cf.* 22:3); morally, he is wilful and irresponsible ("the waywardness of the simple shall slay them", 1:32).'[10] Chapter 7 shows the 'simple' most clearly, 'a young man without sense' (7, RSV), easily enticed down the road to temptation. 'He is a person

[10] Kidner, *Proverbs*, p. 39.

whose instability could be rectified, but who prefers not to accept discipline in the school of wisdom (1:22–32).'[11]

We should also note that 'without sense' is literally 'lacking heart'; and the 'heart' here is a focus of thoughtfulness. 'Lacking heart' means an inability to take a thoughtful view, hence NIV's *a youth who lacked judgment.*

The *fool* is rather more obstinate and stubborn. There are three different Hebrew words in Proverbs translated 'fool', but their meanings overlap. Kidner says of the most common word that the fool 'has no idea of a patient search for wisdom: he has not the concentration for it . . . but imagines it can be handed out to him over the counter. . . The root of his trouble is spiritual, not mental.'[12] The bottom line is that he does 'not choose to fear the LORD' (1:29). He is a social menace, and a source of sorrow to his parents (17:12; 18:6; 13:20; 17:21). Of the other Hebrew words translated 'fool', one adds a 'darker' tone, and emphasizes his 'moral insolence', the other adds an 'extra weight of boorishness'.[13]

The third character is the *scoffer*, who demonstrates that it is 'mental attitude, not mental capacity', that matters. 'He shares with his fellows their strong dislike of correction (9:7, 8; 13:1; 15:12), and it is this, not any lack of intelligence, that blocks any move he makes towards wisdom (14:6).'[14]

The way of Wisdom or the way of Folly?

Chapter 9 brings to an end the opening section of the book of Proverbs. In many ways it is a summary and conclusion of the previous eight chapters. The first section (1–6) is another celebration of Wisdom, and the feast she herself provides. The final section (13–18) is a portrait of the other woman, Folly, who offers only stolen food (9:17). The chapter draws the contrast most starkly.

The contrast is between Wisdom (1–6), who *has built her house* (1), *prepared* her food and *wine* (2) and *sent out* her *maids* with invitations to the party (3–6), and Folly (13–18), who also issues an invitation to her home (15–16), with enticements of food and drink (17). However, Wisdom's guests are helped into *the way of understanding* (6), whereas Folly's table is attended by people who do not realize they are still stupid (18). Between these vignettes come the verses about the mocker to which we have already referred (7–9), and a return to the central and overarching theme of the fear of the LORD (10–12). A brief comparison of Wisdom (1–6) and Folly (13–18) is a good way for us to bring our discussion of these chapters to a close.

[11] *Ibid.*   [12] *Ibid.*, p. 40.   [13] *Ibid.*, p. 41.   [14] *Ibid.*, pp. 41–42.

Wisdom has built her house;
  she has hewn out its seven pillars.
²She has prepared her meat and mixed her wine;
  she has also set her table.
³She has sent out her maids, and she calls
  from the highest point of the city.
⁴'Let all who are simple come in here!'
  she says to those who lack judgment.
⁵'Come, eat my food
  and drink the wine I have mixed.
⁶Leave your simple ways and you will live;
  walk in the way of understanding.'

¹³The woman Folly is loud;
  she is undisciplined and without knowledge.
¹⁴She sits at the door of her house,
  on a seat at the highest point of the city,
¹⁵calling out to those who pass by,
  who go straight on their way.
¹⁶'Let all who are simple come in here!'
  she says to those who lack judgment.
¹⁷'Stolen water is sweet;
  food eaten in secret is delicious!'
¹⁸But little do they know that the dead are there,
  that her guests are in the depths of the grave.

Both women call to the *simple* (4, 16) to come to their house to eat
and drink with her (1, 5, 14, 17). We need to be careful, for the word
translated 'simple' really has a moral tone to it. Toy suggests that in
contrast to those who have understanding, the 'simple' are 'those
who have no moral insight and power of self-direction, the negative,
unformed minds, not yet given up to sin, but in danger of becoming
its dupes'.[15] Both women offer rewards (6, 17). But to come into the
house which Wisdom herself built is to find life and to *walk in the
way of understanding* (6). To heed the call of undisciplined and
ignorant Folly is to remain in one's ignorance (18), and to find
oneself in the place of the *dead*. As with much of Proverbs 1 – 8, we
are faced with a choice.

Hubbard's comments are worth quoting in full:

Like the last movement of a sonata or symphony, this final chapter
of the wisdom speeches recapitulates the major motifs of chapters
1 – 8. It pits Lady Wisdom (vv. 1–6) and Dame Folly (vv. 13–18)

---

[15] Toy, p. 186.

against each other in language that is unmistakably parallel. The issues of choice that have dotted every page and virtually every paragraph are here made starkly clear. They are nothing less than life (v. 6) or death (v. 18).[16]

> Strong Son of God, immortal Love,
>   Whom we, that have not seen thy face,
>   By faith, and faith alone embrace,
> Believing where we cannot prove.
>
> Thine are these orbs of light and shade;
>   Thou madest Life in man and brute;
>   Thou madest Death; and lo, thy foot
> Is on the skull which thou hast made.
>
> Thou wilt not leave us in the dust:
>   Thou madest man, he knows not why;
>   He thinks he was not made to die;
> And thou hast made him: thou art just.
>
> Thou seemest human and divine,
>   The highest, holiest manhood, thou;
>   Our wills are ours, we know not how;
> Our wills are ours, to make them thine . . .
>
> Forgive these wild and wandering cries,
>   Confusions of a wasted youth;
>   Forgive them where they fail in truth,
> And in thy wisdom make me wise.

> Alfred, Lord Tennyson, from the beginning of
> *In Memoriam A. H. H.* (1850)

[16] Hubbard, p. 128.

Part 3
Wisdom's methods

We will pause at this point to stand back from Proverbs and ask ourselves some questions about how its writers go about their work. This is not the way of doing theology we find in St Paul's letter to the Romans. Nor is this like the histories of the Pentateuch or the narrative of the gospels. Proverbs are not stories or prophecies or letters. There are questions here about theological method and literary style. This chapter will explore some of these questions and, I hope, will serve as a sort of introduction to our next section, where we look in more detail at Proverbs 10 – 22.

The theology of lived experience

In some of the pressing personal struggles for Christian people today, there often seems to be a dichotomy between the teachings of the faith and the actual experience of living in God's world. It may have been like that 150 years ago when William Wilberforce was striving to persuade fellow church people that the slave trade was evil and should be abolished. But did not the Old Testament sanction slavery? Did not St Paul tell slaves how to behave in relation to their masters? The Bible did not say anything about the abolition of slavery, an essential institution for the growth of the nineteenth-century capitalist economy, which had itself derived from the Christian values of thrift, hard work and a duty to serve God whatever one's station in life. This was how some of the reasoning went. But for Wilberforce, and no doubt for Christian slaves, the received teachings did not fit with their experience. Was it that their experience of longing for freedom needed to be called in question by the tradition of faith? Did they need to learn a new obedience to the teachings of the Scriptures? Or was it that the traditional way of interpreting the Scriptures needed to be looked at again in the light of human experience?

In fact, of course, for us the word 'slavery' is inevitably coloured by the evils of the European, Caribbean and American slave trade. In the

Old Testament, the situation of the slave was somewhat different. Indeed, in respect of Hebrew practice, the word 'slave' as commonly understood was hardly applicable at all, for the slave or servant was a member of the extended family, protected by membership of the covenant community (*cf.* Gn. 17:13). The distinctiveness of this social institution is seen when we realize that the most extended piece of legislation about slaves in the Old Testament was concerned with slaves who did not wish their slavery to end (Ex. 21:1–6). Even in St Paul's day, alongside the desperate cruelty towards slaves in some of Greek and Roman society, there was still the general sense that a slave was valuable property to be protected. That is not to say that the full expression of the Christian gospel does not include the abolition of a practice in which one human being owns another as property – of course it must. But what is called in question is the simple movement from the biblical text to contemporary decisions. Even in the matter of slavery, there is some careful cultural translating to do. The evil trade in slavery in its cruel eighteenth-century form required a fresh reappraisal of what Old and New Testaments said about slaves in the light of this new experience.

Some parts of the church are going through a similar process in relation to changing understandings of human sexuality. Sixty years ago, the Church of England bishops were very unhappy about contraception. Christian people are divided over the question whether divorce is sometimes, though a tragic last resort, none the less a responsible choice in a situation of personal hurt and destructiveness. Can women exercise a position of authority and leadership within the church? In these and many other ways, Christian people have been faced with the task of applying their theology, learned as doctrines or dogmas, to the new questions raised for them by the experiences and struggles of living in new situations. Their answers are not all the same.

As part of this process, Christian people have been faced with the question of theological *method*. Many have been inspired by the struggles of Christian people in Latin America in their rejection of the traditional western method of applying doctrine to practice. Theology, they argued, should be done the other way round. We do not simply get our doctrine 'straight' and then apply it to the business of living. Rather, we try to be as honest as we can about understanding our experience of living, and, by critical reflection on our practice, we develop and refine our ways of speaking about God. Liberation theology takes its rise from the struggles for social and political liberation in Central America. What some theologians have called 'critical theological reflection on praxis' – and what we might summarize as 'trying to understand our experience in the light of our theology, and rethinking our theological language in the light of our experience' – has given the church a different method of speaking about the ways of God and how life should be lived in God's world.

In fact, many Christians are now realizing that the task of doing the sort of theology which relates to daily living is an ongoing conversation between doctrine and practice, received tradition and contemporary experience. We need to know what God said *then*, in the lives, history and experiences of God's people, and we need to find ways of expressing what God says *now* through what he said then, in our lives, our histories and our experiences. It is not a simple matter of 'doctrine' or 'experience'. What we need is in fact a 'practical theology'.

In some ways these questions of theological method can be paralleled by changes in the worlds of moral philosophy and education. I have explored these in more detail in the appendix to this chapter. To summarize what is discussed more fully there, some philosophers are recovering what earlier writers used to call 'practical reasoning': that is, a means of discovering what is true about the world through thinking about experience. Similarly, some who work in the field of education have developed an understanding of the processes of education which involves a conversation between received information and lived experience.

This is not very far at all from what is going on in Proverbs. Ordinary human actions and experiences are brought into the light of faith in God, and the reader is asked to make connections between the two. Some of the proverbs, for instance, face us with the question of what we are doing. 'The wise woman builds her house, but with her own hands the foolish one tears hers down' (14:1). The question thus comes to me: am I building or tearing down? They then place these actions in the context of certain values and visions of life: is my behaviour characteristic of 'the wise' or 'the foolish'? And underlying all this is the religious Story of the ways of God and his purposes for the world. 'He whose walk is upright fears the LORD' (14:2). The effect of the proverb is to bring our actions and values into the light of the Story of God and provoke a conversation between the two. Its purpose is to make us have that conversation, and to move us to new action in a new light.

'An anthology of gnomes'

As we move into a consideration of the specific proverbs of chapters 10 – 31, we are immediately struck by the variety of themes, and apparently haphazard placing of the material. Proverbs about being wise and fearing God seem to sit oddly next to proverbs about gossippy men or contentious women. Laziness is referred to in the verse adjacent to one about inheriting property; violence, guilt, innocence, bribery, mockery and love of wine are interwoven with verses about justice, going to war, generosity, child discipline, and an honest answer being like a kiss on the lips.

Clearly here is a collection; what Toy in his commentary (quoting Bruch) refers to as 'an anthology of gnomes'.[1] A 'gnome', or a gnomic saying, is a wise aphorism which captures a scene, an attitude or an action, and invites the reader to reflect on it. As an anthology, there is no particular order to it; it is more to be dipped into than read consecutively. Perhaps its jumbled-up aspect is even a deliberate ploy to reflect life as it is!

Some of the material clearly reflects a style of life and social setting very far removed from most – certainly western – Christian people at the dawn of the third millennium. So can 'the message of Proverbs' make much sense to us? Can this material prove to have some use in helping us live for Christ in our very different world?

Fourfold structure

One of the literary techniques which many of the proverbs use, and of which we must be aware if we are to answer that question, is the use of a fourfold structure.

According to T. A. Perry,[2] this 'quadripartite form' is typical of much of the wisdom writing of the ancient Middle East. Much of what follows in the next few paragraphs is derived from his work. Perry argues that to recognize this form is to gain an insight into the way many of the proverbs 'work', and how, through them, the wise men were able to analyse and pass on certain cultural values. The basic assumption of Perry's work is the very reasonable one that proverbs are assertions of value. Certain things are good, others bad. What the fourfold structure (or, better, four-line formation) does is to bring these values to light, and help us to put priorities on them.

Some of the Proverbs are explicitly 'better . . . than' proverbs. For example: 'Better a meal of vegetables where there is love than a fattened calf with hatred' (15:17). We could characterize this proverb in these key phrases:

> Make do with vegetables and experience love.
> Have meat and experience hatred.

There are four elements involved in this proverb: on the one hand, vegetables and meat, and on the other love and hatred. The proverb assumes (with apologies to vegetarians) that vegetables are a lesser

---

[1] Toy, p. x.
[2] Perry, taking further some of the work of G. B. Milner.

good than meat; and we would all agree that hatred is less desirable in life than love. If we call the less good and the less desirable 'negative' (−), and the more desirable 'positive' (+), the proverb then looks like this:

> Make do with vegetables and experience love (−, +).
> Have meat and experience hatred (+, −).

Perry's analysis indicates that there is a deeper implied structure in this proverb. There is also a (+, +) and a (−, −). We could express them like this:

> Have meat and experience love (+, +).
> Make do with vegetables and experience hatred (−, −).

The proverb in this case is just the middle two terms of the fourfold structure, in which we recognize that there are positive values like meat and love, and negative values such as making do with vegetables and hatred. The proverb forces us to consider our relative values. What matters most to us, meat or love? Are we willing to make do without certain things that otherwise are good (such as meat), and cope with what is less than the best in the food line (such as managing with only vegetables) in order to find the best, namely love?

Some proverbs seem to express a simple preference. To take a different example: 'A good name is more desirable than great riches.' This is reinforced in the next line: 'to be esteemed is better than silver or gold' (22:1). It seems to speak only of a good name and riches, but underneath there is the fourfold structure again:

> riches and a good name (+, +)
> poverty and a good name (−, +)
> riches and a bad name (+, −)
> poverty and a bad name (−, −)

By uncovering this structure we realize that the writer is not only saying that riches and a good name are both desirable, but is forcing us to focus on their relative values: a good name is to be preferred even when it entails poverty.

Sometimes the pithiness of the proverb implies more than is said. For example: 'A wise son brings joy to his father, but a foolish son grief to his mother' (10:1). Surely this does not suggest that the wise son does not also bring joy to his mother, and the foolish son grief to his father? On our valuation grid we could perhaps suggest:

> A wise son brings joy to both parents (+, +).
> A foolish son brings grief to both parents (−, −).

The two missing terms would then be

> A wise son brings grief to both parents (+, −).
> A foolish son brings joy to both parents (−, +).

The apparent absurdity of such statements comes from our habit of reading them as though 'wise' implies 'brings joy to' and 'foolish' implies 'brings grief to'. But it is surely possible for foolish sons to do things which bring joy (as Esau brought joy to Isaac); and for parents to take delight in things which are not wise. The proverb is asking sons to reflect on what will bring joy and what will bring grief, and asking parents to reflect on whether they take delight in wisdom or foolishness.

Within the book of Proverbs there are many sayings in which one topic refers to physical or worldly things, and the other refers to spiritual or religious values. For instance: 'Better a dry crust with peace and quiet than a house full of feasting, with strife' (17:1). Here the spiritual value of peace is put alongside the worldly value of feasting. Sometimes the spiritual values contradict or call in question the physical values. Many of the proverbs are in fact structured to expose the importance of spiritual values and ask the reader to evaluate his own values in their light. For instance: 'Better a patient man than a warrior, a man who controls his temper than one who takes a city' (16:32). The warrior and the one who takes a city are both presented as positive values, but they are this-worldly values, and the proverb relativizes them. The spiritual values of patience and of controlling one's temper are more important even than the skills of the soldier.

Not all the proverbs of chapters 10 – 31 fall into this pattern, but a great many do, especially those with a 'better. . . than' structure. The benefit of exposing the pattern wherever it is present is that it forces us to make comparisons between values: not only what is good and what is bad, but, more especially, what is better and what is worse. The latter task is helped by the (+, −) and (−, +) sentences in the middle of the fourfold structures.

Several writers have searched the book of Proverbs for lists of the basic values underlying the culture of the wisdom schools. Perry, for example, lists work, fear of God, love, righteousness, lowliness of spirit, slowness to anger, quiet (peace), integrity, openness, nearness and wisdom.[3]

In our next section, we will build on these suggestions, and try to illustrate many of the underlying values of Wisdom. As we said

---

[3] He also quotes Crenshaw as linking these with the four cardinal virtues of Egyptian wisdom, namely timeliness, integrity, restraint and eloquence. Perry, p. 42.

earlier, some of the detail of many of the proverbs feels very out of place in the twentieth century. Perhaps, however, it will be a salutary exercise for us to uncover some of Wisdom's values. We need to bring our stories into line with Wisdom's Story, test our vision in the light of Wisdom's vision, and allow our values to be called in question by Wisdom's values. That is one of the ways the message of Proverbs can still strike home to us, and open to us rich resources of practical wisdom.

Wisdom's imagination

One of the most marked differences between the wisdom literature and other styles of writing in the Bible is Wisdom's use of vivid word pictures. In the opening chapter, for example, we saw a powerful vignette depicting a gang plotting a mugging. The youth is being enticed by the group: 'Come along with us, let's lie in wait for someone's blood, let's waylay some harmless soul; let's swallow them alive, like the grave, and whole, like those who go down to the pit; we will get all sorts of valuable things and fill our houses with plunder' (1:11–13) Later we saw how the allurements of the adulteress are graphically described: the lattice window, the street corner at twilight, the kiss, the bed, the perfumes, the absent husband, the persuasive words (7:6–23). Wisdom herself is portrayed in pictures: the town crier on the street corner, the house-builder. And creation itself is painted in rich and evocative colours (8:22–30).

But there is another aspect, too, to Wisdom's rich imagination: the use of simile and metaphor in the wise sayings. This, as we shall see, is especially true of those collected together in some of the later chapters of Proverbs. It is the surprise of the vivid metaphor which shocks us and shakes us, and makes the point. Here are some examples.

Several times, the priceless value of wisdom, knowledge and understanding is compared to that of jewellery which adorns the head and the neck: 'She is more profitable than silver and yields better returns than gold. She is more precious than rubies' (3:14–15).[4]

When the young man is being cautioned against the loose women, and reminded of the need to keep himself within appropriate moral bounds, the teacher uses the powerful image of the water cistern:

---

[4] Notice also: 'They will be a garland to grace your head and a chain to adorn your neck' (1:9); '. . . an ornament to grace your neck' (3:22); 'She will set a garland of grace on your head and present you with a crown of splendour' (4:9); 'Gold there is, and rubies in abundance, but lips that speak knowledge are a rare jewel' (20:15); 'The crucible for silver and the furnace for gold, but man is tested by the praise he receives' (27:21); 'A word aptly spoken is like apples of gold in settings of silver' (25:11); 'Like an ear-ring of gold or an ornament of fine gold is a wise man's rebuke to a listening ear' (25:12).

'Drink water from your own cistern, running water from your own well. Should your springs overflow in the streets, your streams of water in the public squares?' (5:15–16).

The erotic pleasure of sexual embrace with the wife of one's youth calls to mind the tenderness and smooth skin of a young deer: 'A loving doe, a graceful deer – may her breasts satisfy you always' (5:19).

Throughout these collections, word pictures of animals are often used to bring proverbs to life: the gazelle, the ant, the pig, bear, birds of various sorts, the horse, the dog and so on.[5] In other places, the weather is the chosen metaphor.[6] In other places again, the comparison is with food, or seasoning, or vinegar.[7]

The quarrelsome wife has various extremely unfavourable comparisons: 'Better to live on the corner of the roof than share a house with a quarrelsome wife . . . Better to live in a desert than with a quarrelsome and ill-tempered wife' (21:9, 19). 'A quarrelsome wife is like a constant dripping on a rainy day; restraining her is like restraining the wind, or grasping oil with the hand' (27:15).

And the worlds of the refiner, the toolmaker, the weapons-maker and the archer are drawn on several times: 'Remove the dross from the silver and out comes material for the silversmith; remove the wicked from the king's presence, and his throne will be established through righteousness' (25:4–5). 'Like a club or a sword or a sharp arrow is the man who gives false testimony against his neighbour' (25:18). 'Like an archer who wounds at random is he who hires a fool or any passer-by' (26:10).

[5] Thus: 'Free yourself, like the gazelle from the hand of the hunter, like a bird from the snare of the fowler' (6:5); 'Go to the ant, you sluggard; consider its ways and be wise!' (6:6); 'Like a gold ring in a pig's snout is a beautiful woman who shows no discretion' (11:22); 'Better to meet a bear robbed of her cubs than a fool in his folly' (17:12); 'Like a fluttering sparrow or a darting swallow, an undeserved curse does not come to rest' (26:2); 'A whip for the horse, a halter for the donkey, and a rod for the backs of fools!' (26:3); 'Like one who seizes a dog by the ears is a passer-by who meddles in a quarrel not his own' (26:17); 'Like a bird that strays from its nest is a man who strays from his home' (27:8); 'Like a roaring lion or a charging bear is a wicked man ruling over a helpless people' (28:15).

[6] 'Like the coolness of snow at harvest time is a trustworthy messenger to those who send him; he refreshes the spirit of his masters' (25:13); 'Like clouds and wind without rain is a man who boasts of gifts he does not give' (25:14); 'Like one who takes away a garment on a cold day, or like vinegar poured on soda, is one who sings songs to a heavy heart' (25:20); 'Like snow in summer or rain in harvest, honour is not fitting for a fool' (26:1); 'A ruler who oppresses the poor is like a driving rain that leaves no crops' (28:3).

[7] 'As vinegar to the teeth and smoke to the eyes, so is a sluggard to those who send him' (10:26); 'Better a meal of vegetables where there is love than a fattened calf with hatred' (15:17); 'Pleasant words are a honeycomb, sweet to the soul and healing to the bones' (16:24).

A variety of different pictures is used to warn the fool, the sluggard, and the easily tempted man. For example: 'Like tying a stone in a sling is the giving of honour to a fool' (26:8); 'Like a thornbush in a drunkard's hand is a proverb in the mouth of a fool' (26:9); 'As charcoal to embers and as wood to fire, so is a quarrelsome man for kindling strife' (26:21).[8]

There is a further important point that needs underlining. Many of the proverbs are rather funny. We are not meant to read Proverbs with too much spiritual seriousness; some of the pictures should provoke a laugh rather than a prayer – or perhaps a laugh which leads to a prayer. The picture of the nagging spouse being compared to a dripping tap on a rainy day is meant to provoke amusement (27:15). There will be wry smiles of recognition when a she-bear without her cubs is said to be more tolerable than the neighbourhood bore (17:12). There will be some embarrassed chuckles at the vivid description of the drunkard in 23:29–35.

This last passage, in fact, serves as a good illustration of Wisdom's rich imagination, and how her vivid pictures serve as an educational tool. The section begins with six questions – a sort of riddle which asks the reader to try to think what sort of person the teacher is thinking of:

Who calls out 'Oh!'?
Who cries out 'Alas!'?
Who gets embroiled in quarrels?
Who is always complaining?
Who gets needless bruises, either by losing his balance, or by getting into a fight?
Who has bloodshot eyes, dull and red, unable to see clearly? (*cf.* 23:29).

Then comes a description of the drunkard, the late drinker who spends his time in drinking bouts, continually going in search of 'mixed wine', specially strengthened with herbs (30). To gaze at full red wine leads immediately, for the drunkard, to craving it. But it is always the same: at first it glides down the throat smoothly, over the

[8] *Cf.* also: 'Like a bad tooth or a lame foot is reliance on the unfaithful in times of trouble' (25:19); 'Like a lame man's legs that hang limp is a proverb in the mouth of a fool' (26:7); 'As a door turns on its hinges, so a sluggard turns on his bed' (26:14); 'Like a madman shooting firebrands or deadly arrows is a man who deceives his neighbour and says, "I was only joking!"' (26:18–19); 'Like a coating of glaze over earthenware are fervent lips with an evil heart' (26:23); 'Though you grind a fool in a mortar, grinding him like grain with a pestle, you will not remove his folly from him' (27:22); 'Can a man scoop fire into his lap without his clothes being burned? Can a man walk on hot coals without his feet being scorched?' (6:27–28).

lips and the palate, but at last it bites like a snake.[9] The drunken stupor (33) and disturbed rest, like that of a seasick person on board ship trying to sleep at the top of a mast (34), mean that even his bruises do not hurt (or perhaps, he does not care about them, 35). Even when he wakes, he will want to get another drink. Habitual drunkenness has led to alcoholism. The poignant picture which draws on humour and vivid imagery is in fact a serious and sombre warning.

Here, then, are some ways into Wisdom's imagination. What does all this add up to?

First of all, this is a reminder, or a renewed emphasis on the fact, that Wisdom is a celebration of ordinary life. Nothing is too small, too ordinary, too matter of fact, to become the vehicle for the teaching of wisdom. The world of creativity in the natural order, the worlds of animals and plants, the world of the artisan and the craftsman, the weather, food and drink – anything, it seems, which fits into the routine of daily living – can become a metaphor, a simile, an analogy or a parable by which God's Wisdom may be appreciated.

Secondly, it is an encouragement to take the imagination seriously. In these days of changing modes of thought (that complex of ideological and cultural upheavals which goes by the name of postmodernism), there is a renewed emphasis on the imagination. Sometimes this arises negatively out of the move from a verbal to an image culture, in television, virtual reality and computer games, and the plea is for a recovery of creative imagination to replace the passivity of the couch potato. Sometimes, though, there is a more positive recognition of the inadequacy of instrumental and technical reason as the basis for our understanding. The Enlightenment heritage, despite all its benefits, has tended to lead to a view of understanding in solely detached, 'scientific' (in the popular sense), rationalistic terms. But now there is thankfully a recovery of the awareness that 'the heart has reasons which reason knows not of'.[10] There is a rediscovery of 'this sunrise of wonder'.[11] There is a new realization of the power of poetry, art and story.

No-one has exhibited the relation between reason and imagination more clearly than C. S. Lewis. His literary criticism and Christian apologetic writing on the one hand, and his *Chronicles of Narnia* on the other, display a tension between reason and imagination which shaped all of his writings. In an early poem about Athena and Demeter, before he became a Christian, Lewis seems to suggest that

[9] See Toy on verses 31–32.
[10] Blaise Pascal, *Pensées*.
[11] To borrow Michael Mayne's title. See p. 16 above.

reason, practical reason, is the ruler of the soul, and its protector against error, whereas imagination is dark and seductive and somewhat dangerous. Peter Schakel illustrates how Lewis's conversion to Christian faith led him on to a road in which imagination and intellect could be reconciled. 'The result was a wholeness, not just in Lewis's writings, but in his life generally . . . he was able to . . . accept the limitations of a totally rational approach, and become a more relaxed and balanced person.'[12]

It is interesting how this harmony is illustrated in Proverbs in the picture of Wisdom, and the imaginative pictures which Wisdom draws. It is also, of course, vividly illustrated in the way Jesus paints word pictures of shepherds and soil, of vine and bread, of muggings and mustard seeds, to illustrate the life of the kingdom of God. In fact, it is highly probable that Jesus is drawing on the style of the wisdom teachers in his more specifically ethical teaching also.[13]

Gradually, this rediscovery of the imagination is finding its way back into the Christian church as well. Of course, we need to be careful. It is quite possible to 'imagine' all sorts of things which have no basis in truth or reality. Imagination is not the same as fantasy – and there are aspects of some contemporary spiritualities which are dangerously fantastic. We need the sure ground of the Word of God to be able to respond to the scepticism illustrated by the question: 'What is the difference between your saying God spoke to you in a dream, and your dreaming that God spoke to you?' The sanctified imagination belongs in harmony with the sanctified intellect as aspects of an integrated personality. Yet this should be no new thing. In the beginning of creation, Wisdom was God's delight, 'the craftsman at his side . . . filled with delight day after day, rejoicing always in his presence, rejoicing in his whole world and delighting in mankind' (8:30–31). And throughout the words of the wise, Wisdom's creative imagination brings her teachings to life.

It is appropriate to conclude these reflections on imagination by referring to the way Walter Bruggemann uses one of the proverbs to illustrate how he gets 'inside' a text.[14] This is part of his concern that in the postmodern world, Christian people need to be able to offer a 'counterdrama' – an alternative Story – to the many destructive 'stories' which make up current secular life. He discusses Proverbs 15:17 (which we have already examined) as an example. 'Better a meal of vegetables where there is love than a fattened calf with hatred.'

Two options are contrasted: vegetables are better than roast beef.

[12] P. Schakel, *Reason and Imagination in C. S. Lewis* (Eerdmans, 1984), p. 181.
[13] *Cf.* A. E. Harvey, *Strenuous Commands: The Ethic of Jesus* (SCM, 1990).
[14] W. Bruggemann, *The Bible and Postmodern Imagination* (SCM, 1993), pp. 87ff.

Vegetables are linked with love, beef with hatred. We are discussing the world of economic and social assumptions that are associated with food. Why does the teacher rule out 'beef with love'? Because beef signifies a fast, affluent way of life. To generate beef takes more energy, more competence, more time, more production. Then Bruggemann lets his imagination play: 'So imagine that "beef with strife" refers to a busy family in which everyone is hustling to the limit. They arrive home for dinner too tired to care much, too exhausted to communicate, too preoccupied to invest in each other. Frayed nerves lead to worry, which leads to tension, and finally tears.'[15]

Bruggemann readily acknowledges that he is 'overreading' the text. But he reckons that what he is describing is 'very close to the mood of the proverb'. The proverb refers to an 'eating disorder' which reflects a social disorder. But the teacher suggests 'a more excellent way'. 'Stop the destructive ambition, pull back from the seductions of affluence, and enjoy the neighbour.'[16]

Our purpose in referring to Bruggemann is not to ask whether his exegesis of the text will stand up to all the interpretation he is putting on it: of course he is elaborating it with imaginary material. But it is precisely because he believes (I think rightly) that his imagination in this case has run with the grain of the proverb – has caught what he calls its 'mood' – that this opens up for us ways of interpreting the material which speak directly to our situation.

> The proverb that looks so innocent is in fact a stunning, poignant assault on a taken-for-granted world. That world is one in which we are endlessly committed to the growth of our wealth and the increase of our standard of living. In that world, if one has resources, one is entitled to acquire and eat anything for which one can pay . . . the Teacher saw that exploitative over-living is damaging not only to our individual bodies, but enormously costly to our family and communal networks.[17]

Here, then, is one example of the way in which Proverbs can be read both as a word to our minds and as a picture-book to stimulate the imagination. As we shall see in Proverbs 10 – 22, both styles in the language of Proverbs are woven inseparably together.

Appendix
A brief note on practical theology, philosophy and education

In moral philosophy there has been a recovery in recent years of the

---

[15] *Ibid.*, p. 88.   [16] *Ibid.*   [17] Ibid., p. 89.

importance of what is called 'practical reasoning'. For a long time, moral philosophy concerned itself with the meanings of words, and what was meant by terms like 'good' and 'right' and 'duty'. The moral reasoning involved was detached from the business of living; it was kept separate from life, rather as some liberation theologians thought traditional western theology was detached and academic. But 'practical reasoning' – which actually goes back as far as Aristotle – is a way of reasoning about the world from reflection on engagement in a particular social setting.

It is worth taking a moment or two to clarify this. Aristotle in fact writes about three ways in which human understanding can arise. He calls them, in the Greek, *theōria, praxis* and *poēsis*. *Theōria* refers to a way of knowing about the world through contemplation, through detached thought. By contrast *praxis* comes from critical reflection on social engagement, and *poēsis* is a way of knowing which comes from making things. They lead respectively to theoretical knowledge (which is an end in itself), to practical knowledge (which helps us to order human affairs), and to productive knowledge (which guides in the construction of things needed for living).

It is the recovery of 'praxis', or practical reasoning, in some moral philosophy and some social science, that is of particular interest to us at the moment. For Aristotle, praxis is concerned with purposeful human conduct, and with social ethics – how people order their lives in their society. The state of mind from which praxis derives is *phronēsis*, the habit of practical wisdom.

And this brings us back to Proverbs. For in the book of Proverbs, there is nothing of the detailed doctrinal argumentation which we find in, for example, Paul's letter to the Romans. There is no application of doctrine, like that illustrated in several of the New Testament letters. The theological method of Proverbs is much nearer the critical reflection of liberation theology, or the *phronēsis* of Aristotle's practical wisdom. Proverbs, in other words, is a masterly textbook of practical theology.

The field of practical theology has itself been undergoing a revival in recent years. Whereas much traditional 'pastoral theology', such as we see in the Reformation tradition, is the application of the doctrines of grace to pastoral practice, 'practical theology' as it has developed in recent decades is in fact a plea for a different sort of theological method. The experiences of Anton Boisen reflecting theologically on his mental breakdown in 1936, written up as *The Exploration of the Inner World*, had a profound effect on the work in pastoral and practical theology in USA, and on the writings of people like Seward Hiltner, Carroll Wise, Wayne Oates and recently Don Browning. Boisen advocated a case-study method, integrating psychological and religious insights in his theological reflection on 'the human document'. From this, practical theology in these authors developed in the direction of what Hiltner called an 'operation-centred' rather than a 'logic-centred' branch of theology – that is, a way of doing theology in the mode of 'the reflective practitioner'. Don Browning's own massive contribution in this field is best accessed through a series of books on pastoral theology published by Fortress Press and his own *A Fundamental Practical Theology*,[18] in which he reframes the whole theological task in the light of the re-emergence in moral philosophy of 'practical reasoning'.

The theological conversation on practice, the reflective practitioner, the reframing of moral questions and religious questions in the light of practical reasoning – these are the sorts of things which we find going on in Proverbs.

Another discipline in which there is continuing debate about method as well as content is of course the field of education. Here again there are contrasting styles for the education of young people. Are children empty vessels into which the wise older people pour their learning? Or are they people whose limited experiences of life can none the less be the starting-points for reflection on experience which can broaden their horizons and lead them into new discoveries? Some of the so-called 'modern methods' in primary education are in fact a recovery of the methods of practical reasoning which the western world had tended to lose sight of in its concentration on more detached and analytical ways of knowing. Of course there is a place for sharing the content of knowledge ('learning their tables'). Of course the capacity for detached analytical reasoning is important. But so is phronesis (the habit of practical wisdom), leading to praxis (reasoned reflection on experience).

One significant writer on Christian education, Thomas Groome,[19] has developed a fivefold model for understanding educational praxis, and his headings illustrate what this approach involves. He begins by 'naming present action'. The focus of attention in this first place is on what we are actually doing, physically, emotionally, intellectually and spiritually as we live on personal, interpersonal and social levels. The questions here are 'What is going on in your life? Can you describe what you are doing?' The focus is on the question 'What?'

Secondly, Groome moves to critical reflection on that action, by asking how it fits into the story and vision of a person's life and

[18] Fortress, 1991.
[19] T. Groome, *Christian Religious Education: Sharing our Story and Vision* (Harper and Row, 1980).

character. Critical reflection is a combination of reason, memory and imagination, and Groome's focus now is on the question 'Why?' 'Why are you doing that? Why does doing that express something of your life story and your vision for human life?'

The third 'movement' in this process is a deliberate shift of focus to 'the Christian community's story and vision'. In other words, the process now includes reflection on and learning from the tradition of Christian thinking and theology which has been handed down to us. This is where doctrine and tradition enter into the conversation.

Fourthly, Groome moves to a 'dialectical hermeneutic', a critical engagement between the person's own story and the Christian Story – that is, the Story of God's purposes revealed in the Bible, centred in Christ, from creation, through covenant and redemption, to the kingdom of his glory. How that Christian Story is understood is subjected to critique in the light of the personal stories which were told at stage two. Those personal stories in turn are subjected to critique in the light of the Christian Story. What does that Story mean for ours? How do our stories respond to it? It is in this coming together of stories that people are able to see their actions and their lives in a new light.

Then, fifthly, the attempt is made to offer a critique of the visions embodied in our present actions in the light of the vision of God's kingdom. How does our present action contribute to the realizing of the vision of God's kingdom? Can we recognize signs of God's work already among us? How can future action be decided upon in the light of the whole process?

Probably the 'five-movement' model is rarely a clear-cut five-stage process of sequential learning. In moments of real practical learning, it is likely that all these edges often get fuzzy, and these five movements may all be involved at once. But the model serves to illustrate different aspects of education, different methods of learning and different techniques for furthering the growth of practical wisdom.

It seems that all these five movements are present in different ways in Proverbs, and, indeed, as we mentioned earlier, in some of Jesus' ethical teaching in the gospels, which fits well with this 'wisdom' tradition.[20]

As an Old Testament education primer, the book of Proverbs uses a variety of methods. There is information to impart, and the 'wise' are certainly not slow in giving counsel. In chapters 1 – 9, we find the regular refrain: 'Listen, my son, to a father's instruction; do not forget my teaching; pay attention to my wisdom.' This is the didactic element in the education given by parents to the young. But there is

[20] *Cf.* Harvey, *op. cit.*

another emphasis, another style, in fact the primary style in the second half of the book (chapters 10 – 31), coming from various sources and perhaps put together at different times, which is much more concerned with learning from experience. The proverbs give us brief pen portraits of life and invite us to see ourselves in them. Some are humorous, some serious, some are critical, some affirming, some polite, some rude; some deal with personal and private attitudes; others are more concerned with social ethics. But by and large they are at one in creating a brief pictorial image, frozen in time like a photograph, and inviting us to place ourselves in the frame, and to learn from the experience and the emotion which that evokes. Their place in the whole book of Proverbs as it has come edited to us, however, invites the readers not only to reflect on those experiences, but to bring them into touch with the Story of God's purposes for his creation, and for humanity within it.

Part 4
Wisdom's values:
Foundations (10:1 – 22:16)

In Parts 1 and 2 we explored the first nine chapters of Proverbs, and then we took a break to discuss some more theoretical matters: Wisdom's methods and imagination. It is now time to return to the text, which we pick up again at the start of Proverbs 10. This is the beginning of a long section which contains a series of collections of different sayings, some of which no doubt are of much earlier origin than some of the material we have already explored. Here are most of the pithy sayings, the 'gnomes', the 'better . . . than' comparisons. Here are many of the vivid images and pictures. We need to be alert to the disjointed nature of these chapters. We will miss the point of some of these sayings if we rush over them as if they were connected prose. It is worth taking time to pause on a particular proverb, rather than reading the whole text in large sections together.

In the last chapter we were seeing that implicit in the way in which many of these proverbs are structured is a certain scale of values. Certain values are more important than others. Sometimes certain core values, often 'spiritual' values, call in question certain other more 'worldly' values. In this chapter we will try to identify some of these core values which underlie the teachings of the wise. What are the central values held by Wisdom herself?

Some of the detailed suggestions may leave us rather cold, if not sometimes morally offended. To be told, for example, that to 'strike a mocker and the simple will learn prudence' does not come easily to western ears today. To be forbidden to remove the ancient boundary mark which was set up by our forefathers does not ring immediate bells with most of us. Our task in the section is not so much to comment on the specific practical teaching itself but rather to uncover the moral values on which such practical teaching is based – in the case of the mocker, the value of prudence and indeed of educative deterrence, and, as we shall see, in the case of the boundary stone, a concern for the rights of the poor.

We begin with the chapters which are brought together under Solomon's name, Proverbs 10:1 – 22:16.

The wise sayings of Solomon

Much of this material can be summarized in two proverbs: 'He who pursues righteousness and love finds life, prosperity and honour' (21:21); and 'Humility and the fear of the LORD bring wealth and honour and life' (22:4).

In other words, to live in the ways of God's righteousness, humbly and reverently in line with his character, and responding to his love, makes for the very best in human flourishing. As we said before, this is always Wisdom's way. If God made the world wisely, and made human beings to be his agents acting wisely in his world, then to find Wisdom is thereby to become truly human.[1] This understanding is also the basis for some of the moral teaching in the book of Deuteronomy. For example, in the exposition of God's law in Deuteronomy 5, the conclusion is, 'Walk in all the way that the LORD your God has commanded you, so that you may live and prosper' (Dt. 5:33). The moral values of Deuteronomy, and indeed the moral values of Wisdom, reflect the moral character of the covenant Lord, Yahweh. So to indicate to human beings who are made in his image that they should reflect these values in their lives and relationships is not a matter of arbitrary imposition of moral obligations; it is much more a statement about what actually makes for the very best for human life and human welfare. This is how we were made.

I remember that in some books of Christian ethics of some years ago, a great deal was often made of 'the Maker's instructions'. If I want to discover how to get the best out of my car, I read the maker's instructions. God's law, it was said, is like that: to be authentically human means to know and live in the way the Maker intended. I was always a little unhappy about this formulation. It seemed to make Christian living only a matter of looking up the manual, tightening the right bolts, and ensuring a regular service. It verged on the legalistic, and missed out on the richness of wonder and mystery in worship, the hard tasks of character formation and growth in vision, and the complicated business of being persons in relationships. But if anywhere in the Bible can lay claim to offer 'the Maker's instructions', I suppose some of these proverbs seem close to a works manual, a list of the bolts to tighten, a checklist for service. Before we look in detail at some of the nuts and bolts, there are three

---

[1] Cf. the way N. T. Wright expresses this in *The New Testament and the People of God* (SPCK, 1992), p. 265.

major themes which present the broad outlines of the model and indicate in general terms how it ought to run: love, justice and, first of all, 'the fear of the LORD'. These, and then the detailed implications of them which we look at in our next section, are what I have called 'Wisdom's values'.

The fear of the LORD

The key text, the motto for the whole of Proverbs, came at the start of the book in 1:7: 'The fear of the LORD is the beginning of knowledge, but fools despise wisdom and discipline.' It came again towards the close of the first section, in 9:10: 'The fear of the LORD is the beginning of wisdom, and knowledge of the Holy One is understanding.' It is a theme which underlies all Wisdom's values.

By 'fear of the LORD' is of course meant 'reverent obedience to Yahweh'. In contrast to an imprisoning fear, often seen in the Old Testament as a consequence of sin (as the man in the Garden says, 'I was afraid', Gn. 3:10), or perhaps in the little boy cowering in the corner, with sticky fingers and a stolen sweet-packet in his hands, the 'fear of the LORD' is, rather, an appropriate response to the authority and enabling power of God. The psalmist indicates that the LORD takes delight in 'those who fear him', and expands the description in terms of 'those who put their hope in his unfailing love' (Ps. 147:11). This 'holy fear', then, carries the sense of an appropriate response to the covenant Lord, who comes to his people in promises of steadfast love and faithfulness, and who is known as the one who rescued his people out of slavery and called them his own. Perhaps this is the sense in which the writer of Ecclesiastes can say that to 'fear God and keep his commandments' is 'the whole duty of man' (Ec. 12:13).

We have all but lost the capacity for reverence – and loss of reverence for God so quickly leads to loss of reverence for people made in his image, and loss of respect for the whole of his creation. In Peter Singer's book on medical ethics,[2] for example, his brazen abandonment of the Judaeo-Christian ethic, which gave us a basis for speaking about the 'sanctity of human life', leads him to regard such a concept as useless. This takes him down a road which not only accepts abortion and euthanasia as a matter of course, but even welcomes infanticide for some unwanted babies and obliges us to value some well-functioning animals as of more value than some disabled humans. I do not find that there is much sense of awe here in the presence of the mystery of the human person. The human person as such is reduced to animal physiology, rational capacity or social utility, and so disappears. How different is the Old Testament

---

[2] Peter Singer, *Rethinking Life and Death* (Oxford University Press, 1995).

recognition that the 'fear of the LORD' leads to an appropriate reverence and respect for what he has made!

This theme, the 'fear of the LORD', is constantly reinforced throughout this second section of the book of Proverbs; for example, several times in chapter 14. The person who fears the LORD is pictured as walking, head held high, on a straight path, knowing where he or she is going, in contrast to someone shiftily dodging behind the trees (14:2). Or the person is depicted as someone secure with his family behind a strong castle wall (14:26): the fear of the LORD casts out other fears. Notice this striking contrast of images in 14:27: 'The fear of the LORD is a fountain of life, turning a man from the snares of death.' A fountain – refreshing, cool, beautiful, life-giving? Or a snare, hidden, entrapping, destructive, the source of pain?

The reiteration of the 'fear of the LORD' is the basic rhythm underneath the whole symphony. Hubbard suggests that 'fear – of – the – LORD' sounds out like the four notes that mark the opening theme of Beethoven's Fifth Symphony.[3] All the rest of chapter 14 is woven around this fundamental motif. There is a great deal in the rest of chapter 14 about personal self-discipline and self-control. For example, the reader must beware of foolish talk (14:3), and instead seek the way of truthfulness (14:5); beware of faithlessness (14:14), and seek the way of prudence (14:15); avoid hot-temperedness (14:17), and seek the way of kindness (14:21). 'A heart at peace gives life to the body', and 'he who is kind to the needy honours God' (14:30–31) – in other words, personal and social health is interwoven throughout this chapter with a reminder about the fear of the LORD. Reverently to obey God is to walk the way of wisdom, which is in fact the way of human flourishing and human health.

As we move to chapter 15, and take a brief glance at this chapter and chapters 16 – 22, the primary compass-bearing once again is 'the LORD'. At one point (15:16), the phrase 'fear of the LORD' is used: 'Better a little with the fear of the LORD than great wealth with turmoil'; but it begins to drop out after that in the rest of these chapters in favour of an emphasis simply on 'the LORD'. The point, however, is not only that all of life is lived under the watchful eye of God, whose eyes are everywhere, seeing the wicked as well as the good (15:3), but that the moral boundaries of God's character determine how he views the lives we lead. So, for example, whereas the LORD is not pleased with 'the sacrifice of the wicked', he is pleased by the prayers of those who are 'upright' (in the right with God) (15:8), and he 'loves' them (15:9). Before God all human hearts 'lie open' (15:11).

[3] Hubbard, p. 198.

The opening section of chapter 16 also focuses on the LORD, with its summary in verse 9: 'In his heart a man plans his course, but the LORD determines his steps.' These verses are almost all 'Yahweh proverbs'. They stress God's sovereignty over human affairs (16:1); he understands human motives (16:2), and rewards those who commit to him whatever they do (16:3). The whole of creation – even the wicked – are governed by God's purposes (16:4). He will punish the proud (16:5), but turns away his punishment from those who are loving and faithful (16:6), and gives them peace (16:7). How much better, then, to live righteously (16:8), under the providential eye of God (16:9). There is blessing for the one who trusts in the LORD (16:20), in whose hand are the ultimate decisions of life (16:33).

Such trust offers a place of safety in an uncertain world. The name of Yahweh is a strong tower which provides safety for those who seek its protection (18:19). It is the LORD's purposes which prevail (19:21), for all human faculties are the gift and creation of God (20:12), and all human steps are ordered by his providence (20:24). His light searches out the human heart (20:27) and weighs it (21:2). Not even the king is exempt (21:1). No wonder that the highest value is to do what is right and just (21:3). 'There is no wisdom, no insight, no plan that can succeed against the LORD' (21:30). Even in battle, although we can get the horse ready, 'victory rests with the LORD' (21:31). Every aspect of life is thus brought into touch with the faith that the Lord is Yahweh.

This is a pattern we find elsewhere in the Old Testament. The Holiness Code, recorded in Leviticus 19, surveys many different areas of life, and appropriate behaviour is indicated because (the refrain comes again and again) 'I am the LORD'; the Lord is Yahweh. Because Yahweh is as he is, there is an appropriate way for his people to live if they are to enjoy his blessing, know his protection, benefit from his care and follow the path which leads to life in his presence. It all stems from Leviticus 19:2, the basic imperative that the Lord's people be like him. Nowhere is this more powerful than in Leviticus 19:18, which tells us to love, because Yahweh is LORD.

Love

We said earlier that the fear of the LORD leads to an appropriate respect and reverence for God and for what God has made. One of the words used in Proverbs to describe that appropriate respect is the word 'love'.

At least two dozen times in these chapters, the writers point to love as being one of the highest of Wisdom's values. The two key Old Testament texts which Jesus uses as his summary of the law of God are the commands to love God with heart and soul and mind and strength (Dt. 6:5), and to love our neighbours as ourselves (Lv. 19:18). These two texts are not only the high points of Old Testament understanding of moral values, but also sum up in themselves all that the rest of the Old Testament law involves. The common caricatures that are so often drawn to contrast the Old Testament and the New, the Old supposedly filled with judgment and wrath and the New centred on love and mercy, are simply untrue. Love is the·highest value of the Old Testament, as in the New, because love is the nature of the covenant Lord. As Charles Wesley's poem has it, 'Thy nature and thy name is Love.'[4] Proverbs stresses the word 'love' and shows what love means in a variety of situations.

We will explore the way Proverbs unpacks something of the meaning of love by looking first at the link between love and faithfulness, then at generosity and friendship, and the link Proverbs forges between love and discipline. Finally we consider the contrast Proverbs draws between love and hatred.

Love and faithfulness

One of the complications of our translations is that there are a number of Hebrew words which are rendered 'love' in English. Sometimes their meanings overlap; sometimes their emphases are different. There is the root 'āhēb, which is mostly the opposite of hatred; it is the love which expresses fondness for something; it is friendship love; it is love directed to a particular object. This is the love referred to in Genesis 27:4, when Isaac speaks of the sort of food he likes; and in Isaiah 56:10, which speaks of dogs who love to sleep. But it is also the word frequently used when our translations offer 'Love God and keep his commandments.' Thus, in Deuteronomy 6:5 we read: 'Love the LORD your God.' The word 'āhēb occurs about twenty times in Proverbs: for example 3:12: 'The LORD disciplines those he loves'; 9:8: 'Rebuke a wise man and he will love you'; 12:1: 'Whoever loves discipline loves knowledge'; and 13:24: 'He who spares the rod hates his son, but he who loves him is careful to discipline him.'[5]

The noun 'ah⁰bâh, which is much less frequent in Proverbs, seems to refer mostly to loving actions. Thus the young man rejoices in the wife of his youth, and is 'captivated by her love' – that is, especially, her attractiveness (5:19). This love 'covers over all wrongs' (10:12; cf. 17:9). It is contrasted with hatred in 15:17. If hidden, it is worse than an open rebuke (27:5). We could summarize the meaning of 'āhēb/ 'ah⁰bâh as 'love with an emphasis on attraction'.

[4] Charles Wesley, 'Come, O thou Traveller Unknown.'
[5] Cf. also 1:22; 4:6; 8:17; 8:21; 15:9; 15:12; 16:13; etc.

The other main word, occurring in Proverbs about ten times, is *hesed*, translated in the RSV 'steadfast love' and in the NIV 'unfailing love' (19:22; 20:6) or 'faithfulness' (3:3; 14:22; 16:6; 20:28; 31:26). It is the love that is linked with righteousness in 21:21. *Hesed* is the word used to describe the character of Yahweh, the covenant Lord. To give one example, the book of Jeremiah, which celebrates the renewal of God's covenant in 31:33, has this earlier saying in verse 3: 'The LORD [Yahweh] appeared to us in the past, saying: "I have loved you with an everlasting love; I have drawn you with loving-kindness [*hesed*]. I will build you up again."'

Covenant love is vividly illustrated by the life story of the prophet Hosea, which is used as a picture of Israel's relationship with God. Hosea is told to marry a woman, Gomer, who then went off after her lovers – just as faithless Israel went off after other gods. Hosea is then told to take her back: 'Go, show your love to your wife again, though she is loved by another, and is an adulteress. Love her as the LORD loves the Israelites, though they turn to other gods' (Ho. 3:1). Interestingly, the word used of Hosea's love in 3:1 is *'āhēb*, though the whole story is an illustration of *hesed*. It is *'āhēb* which brings a couple to marriage. It is *hesed* which sustains it for better, for worse, for richer for poorer, until death. The faithful persistence of God's love – even 'love although' or 'love in spite of' – is translated in the New Testament by *agapē*, and is seen embodied in the New Testament in Jesus who, we are told, even on the night on which he was betrayed, loved his disciples 'to the last' (Jn. 13:1, mg.). 'This is love: not that we loved God, but that he loved us and sent his Son as an atoning sacrifice for our sins' (1 Jn. 4:10).

The love which reflects God's love is a faithful love which persists 'although . . .', a love which is sustained 'in spite of . . .' *Hesed* is 'love in the will', as contrasted with 'love in the heart' (*'āhēb*), which stems from a covenant commitment. This is the love made in the marriage vows. It stays, it persists, through fluctuations of feelings, and variations in the worthiness of its recipient. *Hesed* love is God's gift of grace. Other loves express friendship, emotion or erotic attraction. These can go up and down. What holds a relationship in love is *hesed*.

Proverbs illustrate the close link between love and faithfulness in 14:22: 'Those who plan what is good find [or "show", mg.] love and faithfulness [or "faithful kindness"].' We have met this phrase before in 3:3: 'Let love and faithfulness never leave you; bind them around your neck, write them on the tablet of your heart. Then you will win favour and a good name in the sight of God and man.' (The word translated 'faithfulness' is *'emet*: it means trustworthiness, fidelity and truthfulness.)

The first picture here is of a person wearing a necklace of love and faithfulness, bound round his neck, not as an amulet or charm to ward off evil, but as a locket or chain which is given as a continual reminder. When Judah meets Tamar in the story in Genesis 38, she asks as a 'pledge' of his commitment his 'seal and its cord' (Gn. 38:18).

The second picture is a reminder of the fact that the Ten Commandments were written on tablets of stone. Here, love and faithfulness are written on the tablet of the heart, an image similar to that used by Jeremiah when he speaks of writing God's law in their hearts (Je. 31:33), and perhaps to Deuteronomy 6:8–9, which refers to the way the people are to remember God's commands:

> Hear, O Israel: The LORD our God, the LORD is one. Love the LORD your God with all your heart and with all your soul and with all your strength. These commandments that I give you today are to be upon your hearts. Impress them on your children. Talk about them when you sit at home and when you walk along the road, when you lie down and when you get up. Tie them as symbols on your hands and bind them on your foreheads. Write them on the door-frames of your houses and on your gates.

Love and faithfulness are appropriate responses both to God and also to our neighbour.[6] It is God's personal character of self-giving faithful love which is made known to us in Jesus Christ. It is that quality of faithful love which is seen in the character of Wisdom in Proverbs.

Love and generosity

One of the ways in which Proverbs indicates that love should be expressed is in active generosity, or its flip side, the avoidance of greed. Several times Proverbs emphasizes the unhappy results of greed: 'A greedy man brings trouble to his family, but he who hates bribes will live' (15:27). The picture here is of an oriental family in which the householder is tempted to use unjust ways to get wealthy. Bribes were frequent, but this proverb notes the social disorder they cause. The opposite of grasping for gain is an attitude of generosity. Similarly, 'An unfriendly man pursues selfish ends; he defies all sound judgment' (18:1).

On the contrary, we learn that love is expressed in unselfishness

---

[6] *Cf* also Pr. 20:6: 'Many a man claims to have unfailing love, but a faithful man who can find?' and 'Through love and faithfulness sin is atoned for; through the fear of the LORD a man avoids evil' (16:6). This applies to the king as to everyone else; 'Love and faithfulness keep a king safe; through love his throne is made secure' (20:28).

and generosity. 'A generous man will prosper; he who refreshes others will himself be refreshed.' Generosity brings blessing (11:25–26). In this sort of generous love, there can therefore be a benefit to the giver as well: 'A gift opens the way for the giver and ushers him into the presence of the great' (18:16). 'Everyone is the friend of a man who gives gifts' (19:6).

I think it was the theologian Paul Ramsey who focused the issue in terms of two key questions. One important question is: 'What is good?' But a characteristically Christian question is even more important: 'Whose good is it to be, mine or my neighbour's?'

Love and friendship

Several times love is linked with that most precious – and often most neglected – of virtues, friendship. According to Ralph Waldo Emerson, 'A friend may well be reckoned the masterpiece of nature.' Everyone, he says, searches for friends. We know how precious a good friendship can be, and how sad it is for someone to be friendless.

As I wrote elsewhere,[7] it is very surprising how little 'friendship' seems to feature in contemporary Christian thinking. One can look through dictionaries of ethics and theology, and find plenty on love and on sex, but little on 'friends'. But when we place this alongside the way the fourth gospel speaks of Jesus' relation to his disciples, this is perplexing. 'I have called you friends,' he says. The word for 'friend' is closely related to the way St John speaks about love, and is contrasted with slavery. 'I no longer call you servants, but I have called you friends' (Jn. 15:15).

> Just as some of the rabbis spoke about Jews as being 'friends of God', so Jesus speaks of disciples as his friends, taken into his confidence, trusting his word, respecting his will, finding in their mutual friendship a response to the love of God. There is a liberty, an intimacy, a mysteriously transcendent and loving quality to friendship. It is most often in friendship relationships to others that we discover who we are in ourselves.[8]

On friendship, Proverbs has some wise things to say, and once again the pictures are colourful: 'A friend loves at all times, and a brother is born for adversity' (17:17). These two statements are in parallel: a true friend is always friendly, not only when the sun is shining, just as a brother is still a brother when things are going badly.

---

[7] Foreword to Alistair Ross, *Understanding Friends* (Triangle, 1993).
[8] *Ibid.*

The sense is slightly different in 18:24: 'A man of many companions may come to ruin, but there is a friend who sticks closer than a brother.' This probably means that there are different sorts of 'friendship'. There is the sort of nominal friendship found among those who seek others' company only in order to exploit it for themselves ('a man of many companions'); such 'friends' bring only disaster. A true friend is there when needed, will stand by you when things are really hard, and can be relied on even more, sometimes, than one's relatives. Happy the person who has such a friend!

This is probably the best point at which to explore further aspects of friendship in the various proverbs of these chapters.

To be a friend means to be trustworthy, and to be able to keep confidences (11:13), to be truthful (14:25), and to build up the neighbour through refreshment, guidance and kindness.[9]

Some of the pictures are taken from the world of farming. When the writer says, 'A generous man will prosper; he who refreshes others will himself be refreshed' (11:25), he is drawing on language used of vegetables and animals. Well-nourished livestock and crops prosper (the word for 'prosper', or 'make fat' is also used in Is. 30:23). He is also thinking of irrigation; just as soil needs watering if it is to produce good crops and animals, so a generous man will be 'watered' as he refreshes others.

Friendship is also seen in kindness to the needy (14:21), in carefulness in opening one's mouth when talking about others (11:12) and in not leading one's neighbour down the wrong paths (16:29).

Love, then, is what is desired (19:22). It is no wonder that love becomes the central word both for the moral teaching of the Old Testament and for the teaching of Jesus (cf. Mt. 22:36–40).

---

[9] We notice also in this connection that the wise are concerned about finding goodwill: 'He who seeks good finds goodwill, but evil comes to him who searches for it' (11:27); 'Fools mock at making amends for sin, but goodwill is found among the upright' (14:9). Closely related to this, we notice that the gaining of respect, and the avoidance of disgrace, are more of Wisdom's values: 'A kind-hearted woman gains respect, but ruthless men gain only wealth' (11:16); 'Good understanding wins favour, but the way of the unfaithful is hard' (13:15). On the other hand, 'When wickedness comes, so does contempt, and with shame comes disgrace' (18:3); 'A good name is more desirable than great riches; to be esteemed is better than silver or gold' (22:1). Giving and receiving joy, through actions, attitudes and words, is also valued highly: 'The prospect of the righteous is joy, but the hopes of the wicked come to nothing' (10:28); 'There is deceit in the hearts of those who plot evil, but joy for those who promote peace' (12:20); 'From the fruit of his lips a man enjoys good things, but the unfaithful have a craving for violence' (13:2); 'A man finds joy in giving an apt reply – and how good is a timely word!' (15:23).

Love and discipline

Sometimes in Proverbs love is linked to the need for discipline, showing that love and forgiveness are not soft. There are hard, often painful choices to be made in the face of wrong, to enable relationships to begin creatively again. 'Bring back the birch!' say the tabloid headlines every now and then. 'Parents approve of smacking'; 'Teacher disciplined for hitting child.' To raise the concept of punishment in a discusson is almost certain to raise the temperature. The 'law and order brigade' concentrate heavily on punishment as desert, and too easily abandon any sense that punishment might be restorative. The 'humanitarian' approaches concentrate so much on deterrence and reformation that the question whether punishment is in fact deserved is too often left unaddressed. The Old Testament is often brought into discussion as an example of an uncaring, retributive approach which all right-minded people must now abandon.

But these are all only partial understandings. It is true that the Old Testament does have a concept of retributive justice. Deuteronomy makes clear that the death penalty is thought to be relevant to all offences in breach of the Ten Commandments, though it is much less clear how often that penalty was activated. Clearly, in very different social conditions (with no high-security prisons available, for example), different practical responses were appropriate at different times for the people of God. But the Old Testament concept of justice in punishment is much richer than the mere word 'retribution' suggests. There is a great deal about parental discipline which may sound harsh (*cf.* Dt. 21:18–19), but there are examples in western culture which err rather on the side of the abandonment of parental responsibility, which is hardly morally better. In Proverbs, for instance, the question of parental discipline, and even corporal punishment, is raised in the context of love: 'He who spares the rod hates his son, but he who loves him is careful to discipline him' (Pr. 13:24).

It is perhaps worth pausing here to point out that the *lex talionis* ('an eye for an eye') is never in the Old Testament a statement of savagery, as it is sometimes portrayed, but of equity. It is always offered as guidance for the judge in determining appropriate sentence, never as a rule for personal reaction. There is no evidence in the Old Testament that the terms of the law were ever carried out exactly (eyes put out, teeth extracted, *etc.*). It functions rather as a vivid statement of the principle of exactitude: the equivalence of crime and penalty. The punishment should be appropriate to the crime. This principle was lost in English law when a person could lose his life for stealing a sheep. It is lost today when judicial ferocity awards a disproportionately harsh sentence (lengthy imprisonment for shoplifting), or when judicial leniency awards a sentence plainly less than a serious offence merits (a short sentence for rape or for causing death through driving under the influence of alcohol). It was up to the judge in Old Testament days – as in ours – to determine how the principle should be applied in any given case.

The writer to the Hebrews picks up the linkage we find in Proverbs between love and discipline, though the experience of hardship which is there equated with discipline does not refer to corporal punishment (Heb. 12:5ff.).

Proverbs emphasizes parental discipline in 13:24, and in 15:5 comments on the folly of the son who spurns such discipline. The one who 'heeds correction shows prudence'.[10]

It may well be that we judge that there are more appropriate ways to exercise parental discipline in our day than corporal punishment. What we learn unmistakably from Proverbs, however, is that parental responsibility includes giving moral boundaries and exercising discipline in regard to them. Part of the task of parenting is to provide children with an environment which offers authority for the development of freedom, and protection as an opportunity for growth.[11] Without adequate parental boundaries, as many primary teachers could tell us, children may become very insecure. Moral boundaries and appropriate discipline are both expressions of love.

Love and hatred

Sometimes, in Proverbs, love is contrasted with hatred, and love is said to 'cover over all wrongs' (10:12). Whereas hatred dwells on strife and exaggerates it, love 'hides transgression' (as the AV translates), not by condoning, but by understanding its roots. As St Paul also comments in 1 Corinthians 13:5–7, love 'keeps no record of wrongs' and 'does not delight in evil'. It is this verse in Proverbs

[10] This theme occurs elsewhere in Proverbs, and it is appropriate to notice some examples now. 'Stern discipline awaits him who leaves the path; he who hates correction will die' (15:10); 'Discipline your son, for in that there is hope; do not be a willing party to his death' (19:18); 'Folly is bound up in the heart of a child, but the rod of discipline will drive it far from him' (22:15). This concern with discipline seems to range from 'correction' ('A mocker resents correction; he will not consult the wise'; 15:12) to the severe discipline which is said to 'purge' the soul. The text of 20:30 is rather complicated; NIV has 'Blows and wounds cleanse away evil, and beatings purge the inmost being.' It possibly means (as Toy suggests): 'Cosmetics purify the body, and blows purify the soul.' As Toy comments, 'The thought of the proverb appears to be that moral evil must be put away by severe chastisement.'

[11] Cf. David Atkinson, *Pastoral Ethics* (Lynx, 1994), ch. 6, 'The Future of the Family', p. 65.

which is quoted in the first letter of Peter: 'Above all, love each other deeply, because love covers over a multitude of sins' (1 Pet. 4:8). The New Testament fills out much more fully the meaning of forgiveness, which not only covers over sins, but provides the means for their penalty to be paid and their hurt to be healed. The same thought is offered the other way round in Proverbs 17:9: 'He who covers over an offence promotes love' (cf. also 19:11). This thought is paralleled by that high point of Old Testament prophecy in the eighth century BC: 'Who is a God like you, who pardons sins and forgives . . . transgression?' (Mi. 7:18). Wisdom extols a love which is merciful, forgiving and re-creative.

Justice

We noted earlier how values such as love, faithfulness, justice and righteousness often merge into one another in the character of the covenant Lord. We also said we need to be clear that when we use the word 'justice' we may be picking up only a fraction of the richness of the concept of the Old Testament. The justice of God is essentially concerned with a way of life for God's people which corresponds with the character of God's righteousness. In a sense, therefore, we must allow our human concepts of justice to be corrected and transformed by what we may call 'divine justice'. Having said that, there is much in Proverbs which gives us insight into what justice means in practice: the justice which is in fact the social and political expression of 'neighbour love'.

Justice and the needs of the poor

One of Wisdom's most persistent concerns is the plight of the poor. There is a very strong summary of Wisdom's concerns in 14:31: 'He who oppresses the poor shows contempt for their Maker.' The crucial point here is that the Maker is the same for the oppressor as for the oppressed. Similarly, 'He who mocks the poor shows contempt for their Maker' (17:5). The oppression of the poor is both a violation of someone who should be respected because he or she bears the image of the Creator, and also an attitude which does not reflect the character of the Creator, who is himself on the side of the poor.

This is closely in line with what some theologians have called God's 'bias to the poor', and to which Karl Barth gave classic expression in a much-quoted paragraph:

The human righteousness required by God and established in obedience – the righteousness which according to Amos 5:24

should pour down as a mighty stream – has necessarily the character of a vindication of right in favour of the threatened innocent, the oppressed poor, widows, orphans and aliens. For this reason, in the relations and events in the life of his people, God always takes his stand unconditionally and passionately on this side and on this side alone: against the lofty and on behalf of the lowly; against those who enjoy right and privilege and on behalf of those who are denied it and deprived of it.[12]

Barth elaborates the connection between God's righteousness and his mercy, and then argues that there follows from this the need in us for a political attitude which is 'decisively determined by the fact that man is made responsible to all those who are poor and wretched in his eyes, that he is summoned on his part to espouse the cause of those who suffer wrong'.[13]

Pope John Paul II picks up the same theme in his Apostolic Letter written in preparation for the year 2000.[14] He describes the year 2000 as 'the Great Jubilee', and notes how the Jubilee features in both Old and New Testaments as a time of liberation for the poor. We can remind ourselves that Leviticus 25:8–55 speaks about the protection offered by a form of land tenure to prevent the accumulation of wealth in the hands of a few, and to ensure a more equitable distribution of resources. Slaves were set free. In Luke 4:18–19, the Jubilee ('the year of the Lord's favour') is linked to 'good news' for 'the poor'. Pope John Paul II picks up these themes when he says:

> *The jubilee year was meant to restore equality among all the children of Israel*, offering new possibilities to families which had lost their property and even their personal freedom. On the other hand, the jubilee year was a reminder to the rich that a time would come when their Israelite slaves would once again become their equals and would be able to reclaim their rights. At the times prescribed by Law, a jubilee year had to be proclaimed, to assist those in need. This was required by just government. *Justice, according to the Law of Israel, consisted above all in the protection of the weak.*[15]

The Pope goes on to suggest ways in which Christian people should prepare for the celebration of the Great Jubilee, within the

---

[12] K. Barth, *Church Dogmatics* II/1 (T. & T. Clark, 1957), p. 387.
[13] *Ibid.*
[14] *Tertio Millennio Adveniente* (Catholic Truth Society, 1994).
[15] *Ibid.*, p. 20 (emphasis in original).

church and within the world, including the encouragement to make a serious effort to cancel Third World debt:

> Thus, in the spirit of the Book of Leviticus (25:8–12), Christians will have to raise their voice on behalf of all the poor of the world, proposing the Jubilee as an appropriate time to give thought, among other things, to reducing substantially, if not cancelling outright, the international debt which seriously threatens the future of many nations.[16]

One of the remarkable features of Jesus' healing ministry is that he often reached out across the divide to those who were outcast and marginalized. He touched the untouchable: the leper, the dead body, the woman with a discharge of blood. Those who were regarded as unclean, unacceptable and on the road to death were the chief recipients of his touch of life.

Mary's song at his birth, the *Magnificat*, celebrates the same fact, as we reminded ourselves in a previous chapter:

> . . . he has scattered those who are proud in their inmost
> thoughts.
> He has brought down rulers from their thrones
> but has lifted up the humble.
> He has filled the hungry with good things
> but has sent the rich away empty.

(Lk. 1:51–53)

Proverbs, in less polished form, held these values also. The writers, in various ways, and using various imaginative pictures, raise their voice on behalf of the poor.

It is the LORD, we are told, who tears down the proud man's house, but who keeps intact the widows' boundaries (*cf.* 15:25). The boundaries were clearly an important safeguard for the rights of the poor to have access to land. We recall how the Torah made 'maintaining land boundaries a fundamental anchor of social policy:'[17] 'Do not move your neighbour's boundary stone set up by your predecessors in the inheritance you receive in the land the LORD your God is giving you to possess' (Dt. 19:14). Proverbs picks up this theme in 22:28–29, where the editor has placed the importance of the landmark alongside a reference to those with technical skills – and therefore access to power – perhaps to underline the fact that the landmark was a protection for the powerless.

---

[16] *Ibid.*, p. 63.
[17] To quote W. Bruggemann, *Interpretation and Obedience* (Fortress, 1991), p. 240.

The theme is picked up also in 23:10–11: 'Do not move an ancient boundary stone or encroach on the fields of the fatherless, for their Defender is strong; he will take up their case against you.' Here the concern is specifically on behalf of those who are socially marginalized and without access to power. The 'Defender' is the *gō'ēl*, the next of kin whose right it is to take as his own all the needs, debts, distresses and so on of his beleaguered kinsfolk. Boaz in the story of Ruth was such a *gō'ēl* (*cf.* Ru. 3:9). Here in Proverbs 23:11, the word is used of God. God is the 'kinsman-redeemer' of the fatherless.

> [He] will not tolerate such violation of land rights, especially if done to the marginal and even if done in socially and legally approved ways. It is striking that on as mundane a matter as land boundaries in the literature of Proverbs, such a role is assigned to God.[18]

The injustices against the poor are reflected again in 18:23: 'A poor man pleads for mercy, but a rich man answers harshly' (which may mean more than simply the bad manners of the upper classes. It may mean – as the prophet Amos indicates so powerfully – that the powerlessness of poverty is reinforced by the uncaring rich). The poor are sometimes shunned even by their relatives, to whom they have become a burden, not to speak of being abandoned by those superficial acquaintances whom they thought were friends (19:7).

The language of 22:16 possibly means that it is gain for someone to give generously to the poor, whereas attempts at bribery lead only to impoverishment. Or perhaps here are two abuses of money: oppressive gain, and over-extravagant gifts. In some cultures the assumption of bribery as the basis of commercial transactions is more widespread than in others. But no society which can in any sense call itself rich can rest at ease with the global economy, the growing rift between rich nations and poor nations, the need for rich nations to keep the poor nations poor, the widespread hunger and malnutrition in a vast proportion of the human population, and the massive and ever-increasing Third World debt. Nearer home, it is ironic that according to some reports, there are London boroughs in which the percentage of average earnings spent on the National Lottery is creeping up – especially when a large jackpot is offered – while at the same time the percentage of average earnings being spent on basic groceries and the sort of essential food needed for healthy living is going down. There are those (not least the organizers and a few 'winners') for whom the lottery has brought much wealth. There are many more for whom the lottery has in fact decreased their well-

[18] *Ibid.*, p. 241. See also below, pp. 147–148.

being. Among these are the many charities whose voluntary donations have been halved, as well as some of the poorer people in the community who are beguiled into the belief that by playing the lottery, at last they have the chance of release from poverty.

We need to hear, personally and nationally, the word of the wise: 'If a man shuts his ears to the cry of the poor, he too will cry out and not be answered' (21:13); 'A generous man will himself be blessed, for he shares his food with the poor' (22:9). And why? 'Rich and poor have this in common: the LORD is the Maker of them all' (22:2).

Justice and economic integrity

The book of Proverbs also underlines the importance of honesty in business deals. We are taken now into the world of commerce (11:1), with the picture of the salesman with two differing weights in his bag, one heavy, one light.[19] We are taken into the world which Amos denounced when he complained of those who 'trample the needy and do away with the poor of the land . . . skimping the measure, boosting the price, and cheating with dishonest scales' (Am. 8:4–5).

Chapter 20 has a number of references to similar themes. For example, we discover that the LORD detests inconsistent weights and measures (20:10, 23). Though the 'food gained by fraud' may 'taste sweet', the fraudster 'ends up with a mouth full of gravel' (20:17). To accept bribes or 'pervert the course of justice' is the way of wickedness (17:23).

The administration of justice itself must be scrupulously honest. Proverbs points out the evils of punishing innocent people (17:26), of partiality (18:5), of corruption at court (19:28) and of giving false witness (21:28; 12:17), and states that the LORD detests the acquittal of the guilty just as much as the condemnation of the innocent (17:15).

In general, Wisdom teaches her pupils to be very careful in business deals (11:15), and honest in pay arrangements (11:18). 'Better a little with righteousness than much gain with injustice' (16:8). The king in particular should embody justice (16:10), since justice is essential to the continuance of his throne (16:12).

Justice, we remind ourselves, is part of the character of God.

---

[19] *Cf.* Dt. 25:13–16: 'Do not have two differing weights in your bag – one heavy, one light. Do not have two differing measures in your house – one large, one small. You must have accurate and honest weights and measures, so that you may live long in the land the LORD your God is giving you. For the LORD detests anyone who does these things, anyone who deals dishonestly.'

Ultimately it is God who executes justice in the world: 'Do not say, "I'll pay you back for this wrong!" Wait for the LORD, and he will deliver you' (20:22). This theme is taken up by St Paul in his letter to the Romans (12:19–21), where, after speaking of the importance of the love which fulfils God's law, he reminds his readers: 'Do not take revenge, my friends, but leave room for God's wrath, for it is written: "It is mine to avenge; I will repay," says the Lord. On the contrary [St Paul continues, quoting Pr. 25:21–22]: "If your enemy is hungry, feed him; if he is thirsty, give him something to drink. In doing this you will heap burning coals on his head." Do not be overcome by evil, but overcome evil with good.'

'When justice is done, it brings joy to the righteous but terror to evildoers' (Pr. 21:15).

Justice, righteousness and personal integrity

There are a large number of proverbs in these chapters which contrast the 'righteous' person with the 'wicked'. We have noted some of them already. By the 'righteous' is meant a person who fears the LORD and so is seeking to live justly in the way of Wisdom. The 'wicked' or 'ungodly' person does not show that reverent obedience to the LORD, but instead seeks his or her own values and own ways. Proverbs paints a number of contrasting portraits. For example: 'The LORD detests the way of the wicked but he loves those who pursue righteousness' (15:9).[20]

Underlying several of the proverbs is that Wisdom value called personal integrity or good character. 'The man of integrity walks securely,' we are told, 'but he who takes crooked paths will be found out' (10:9).[21] Wisdom thus urges her pupils to avoid evil ways (*cf.* (17:11–13). What should be sought is honesty, integrity, truthfulness

[20] *Cf.* also the following: 'The LORD does not let the righteous go hungry but he thwarts the craving of the wicked' (10:3); 'Blessings crown the head of the righteous, but violence overwhelms the mouth of the wicked' (10:6); 'The memory of the righteous will be a blessing, but the name of the wicked will rot' (10:7); 'The mouth of the righteous is a fountain of life, but violence overwhelms the mouth of the wicked' (10:11); 'The plans of the righteous are just, but the advice of the wicked is deceitful' (12:5); 'No harm befalls the righteous, but the wicked have their fill of trouble' (12:21). In chapter 13 we discover that 'The righteous hate what is false, but the wicked bring shame and disgrace' (13:5). *Cf.* 'Evil men will bow down in the presence of the good, and the wicked at the gates of the righteous' (14:19); 'The house of the righteous contains great treasure, but the income of the wicked brings them trouble' (15:6).

[21] *Cf.* also: 'The integrity of the upright guides them, but the unfaithful are destroyed by their duplicity' (11:3); 'The LORD detests men of perverse heart, but he delights in those whose ways are blameless' (11:20); 'Whoever trusts in his riches will fall, but the righteous will thrive like a green leaf' (11:28); 'A good man obtains favour from the LORD, but the LORD condemns a crafty man' (that is, a person given to wicked devices) (12:2).

and purity.[22] We are back now to the theme with which we began: the sort of life which God requires, the sort of obedience reflected in the phrase 'the fear of the LORD'. Many of these proverbs have illustrated what that obedience means in terms of neighbour love, the quest for justice, a bias towards the poor, and the need for personal integrity.

Sometimes the proverbs are straightforward. Sometimes, though, their style and message seem contradictory or confusing. Some of Proverbs' assertions seem to be statements of fact, rather like the great affirmations of Psalm 1:1–3, 6. On looking at them they seem all too often to be very far from true to our present experience. This is particularly so in the case of those who suggest that those who fear the LORD and who live righteously will be blessed and will prosper. We need look no further than several other psalms, though, to find a rather different tone. In Psalm 73, for example, the psalmist wonders why the wicked seem to be getting away with everything. Has the righteous person kept himself clean all in vain? Is God really on the side of the godly? It takes a visit to the sanctuary of God before he sees everything in a different light. In the light of eternal values, he discerns the real and eternal wealth of the godly people, in the light of which the wicked are seen to be on the road to death (Ps. 73:23ff.). In the light of this, we remind ourselves that Psalm 1 is more a statement of faith: something affirmed even when – or perhaps especially when – God seems not to be watching over our ways (Ps. 1:6). When the ceiling falls in, or we fail the exam, when cancer is diagnosed, or we are made unexpectedly redundant, Psalm 1 affirms

[22] *Cf.* also: 'The LORD detests lying lips, but he delights in men who are truthful' (12:22); 'Righteousness guards the man of integrity, but wickedness overthrows the sinner' (13:6); 'A truthful witness does not deceive, but a false witness pours out lies' (14:5); 'The wisdom of the prudent is to give thought to their ways, but the folly of fools is deception' (14:8); 'The LORD detests the thoughts of the wicked, but those of the pure are pleasing to him' (15:26); 'The crucible for silver and the furnace for gold, but the LORD tests the heart' (17:3); 'A man of perverse heart does not prosper; he whose tongue is deceitful falls into trouble' (17:20); 'The righteous man leads a blameless life; blessed are his children after him' (20:7); 'Who can say, "I have kept my heart pure; I am clean and without sin"?' (20:9); 'Even a child is known by his actions, by whether his conduct is pure and right' (20:11); 'The way of the guilty is devious, but the conduct of the innocent is upright' (21:8); 'He who loves a pure heart and whose speech is gracious will have the king for his friend' (22:11). How important therefore for the reader to 'guard his soul': 'In the paths of the wicked lie thorns and snares, but he who guards his soul stays far from them' (22:5). The life of righteousness will lead to a good memorial: 'The memory of the righteous will be a blessing, but the name of the wicked will rot' (10:7). It is even assumed that righteousness will lead to long life, whereas it is thought that the wicked will perish young. Other parts of Scripture show that this is not always the case. But once again, the vivid imagery makes us sit up and take note. Even grey hair can be a sign of character: 'Grey hair is a crown of splendour; it is attained by a righteous life' (16:31).

our faith – God is watching over us. Psalm 73 reminds us of how it feels.

We need to be careful, therefore, in reading Proverbs: it really does not always work out quite as matter-of-factly as Proverbs suggests. There is often another side to the picture. We sometimes need to place things in the light of eternal values. But then we need to remind ourselves what the proverbs are. They are not so much statements of fact as educational devices. In pithy, memorable sayings, they jolt us into thinking of things in a new way. In fact, within the book of Proverbs itself, there are many examples where different verses seem on the face of it to assert different things. However, just as in English proverbs we speak of many hands making light work, and yet at the same time know that too many cooks spoil the broth, so in these Hebrew proverbs we do not look for statements so much as for inspiration, insight, and a jolt out of our usual ways of thinking. They ask us to place ourselves in the proverb: is my life being affected in the ways suggested or not? Am I on the side of the wicked or the righteous? Am I in the right with God, or is God against me? Where do I stand in the light of eternity?

Character: a summary

Proverbs, then, displays values for healthy living. The 'fear of the LORD', love and justice are the heart of Wisdom's way. To walk this way is to live the life which reflects the wisdom of God.

Such a person, we might say, is a 'person of character'. His or her life is marked by qualities which are widely respected: truthfulness, faithfulness, love, justice. 'Integrity' comes from the root meaning 'whole' – suggesting a complete person. Wisdom's values provide the foundation on which godly character is built.

One of the callings of Christian people is so to grow up into Christ that we may be mature in him (Eph. 4:13). St Paul expresses his purpose as a minister of the gospel as being to proclaim Christ, 'admonishing and teaching everyone with all wisdom, so that we may present everyone perfect in Christ. To this end I labour, struggling with all his energy, which so powerfully works in me' (Col. 1:28–29).

How is such Christian character grown? It grows in response to the love of God, and therefore it grows in the corporate fellowship of the Christian community, for it is 'with all the saints' that we comprehend something of the height and depth of God's love (Eph. 3:18). It grows by practising Christian obedience. The 'mature' are described as 'those who by constant use have trained themselves to distinguish good from evil' (Heb. 5:14). It is essentially a gift from God we are invited to receive: 'It is because of [God] that you are in

Christ Jesus, who has become for us wisdom from God – that is, our righteousness, holiness and redemption' (1 Cor. 1:30).

It was St Thomas Aquinas who gave theology the concept of 'the fundamental option of the ultimate end'. Commenting on this, Bernard Häring writes:

> Only if a person knows where to go in his journey can he study the possible ways that take him there. From a clear option for 'life in Christ Jesus' there arises a creative liberty and fidelity that give shape to my character, my posture, my attitudes, my actions and the kind of human relationships I shall have.[23]

Proverbs says much the same, though necessarily referring to Wisdom rather than (as Häring does) to Jesus – in whom, centuries later, God's Wisdom is seen.

Love

> Immortal Heat, O let thy greater flame
>   Attract the lesser to it: let those fires,
>   Which shall consume the world, first make it tame;
> And kindle in our hearts such true desires,
> As may consume our lusts, and make thee way.
>   Then shall our hearts pant thee; then shall our brain
>   All her inventions on thine Altar lay,
> And there in hymns send back thy fire again:
> Our eyes shall see thee, which before saw dust;
>   Dust blown by wit, till that they both were blind:
>   Thou shalt recover all thy goods in kind,
> Who wert disseised by usurping lust:
>   All knees shall bow to thee; all wits shall rise,
>   And praise him who did make and mend our eyes.

George Herbert

---

[23] B. Häring, *Timely and Untimely Virtues* (St Paul, 1986), p. 28.

Part 5
Wisdom's values:
The practical dimension (10:1 – 22:16)

It is now time to concentrate on some of the more practical dimensions of the life of wisdom. Love, justice, integrity and the fear of the LORD are not abstract ideas which float above us in some ethereal cloud. They have earthly cash value in terms of personal relationships, attitudes, needs and fears. Some psychologists speak of a 'hierarchy of human needs'. In his *Toward a Psychology of Being*,[1] for example, Abraham Maslow 'postulates that all human beings have a hierarchy of basic needs, beginning with the "lower" needs of food, drink, sleep, shelter and clothing, and ascending through such requirements as a sense of belonging, friendship and self-esteem to the "higher" needs of personal fulfilment, an integral system of values and an aesthetic dimension to life'.[2] Other psychologists have slightly different lists. Erikson, for example, stressed the need for trust and mutuality, for a meaningful sense of identity, and for the integrity of accepting the ultimacy of one's life cycle. Otto Rank emphasized the opposite fears of life and of death, and explored the tension between the need to accept one's individuality and the need to be loved and accepted by others.

The work of some theologians can also be analysed in terms of their concern for basic human needs, which tend to be expressed more in terms of the need for God's grace (Augustine), the restoration of relationship with God (Jonathan Edwards), or love which casts out anxiety or despair (Kierkegaard).[3] We have noticed in our earlier chapters how some of these human and spiritual needs feature in the book of Proverbs, and we concentrated in our last chapter on love, justice and integrity. Now we are going to look

[1] Van Nostrand, 1968.
[2] From Roger Hurding's summary of Maslow in Hurding, *Roots and Shoots* (Hodder and Stoughton, 1985), p. 150.
[3] A summary is provided in Ken Boa, 'Theological and Psychological Accounts of Human Needs: A Comparative Study' (D.Phil thesis, Oxford, 1994), from which some of my phrasing in this sentence is taken.

more at some of the very practical and earthy values expressed in Proverbs 10 – 22, which, as we shall see, reflect some of the human needs of which psychologists like Maslow speak.

Wisdom's values include the importance of family, marriage and parenthood, the significance of the opportunity to work and the value of hard work, the importance of good health and of a sense of security, the benefit of material sufficiency, the importance of guarding the tongue in the way we speak to others, and the need for political vision in the wider society. Some of these values are applied very particularly to the life of the king and the royal court. Most are addressed to ordinary people. All in all, they add up to a vibrant celebration of life, freedom and hope, even in the face of death; and stress the importance of the quest for knowledge and understanding. We will try to unpack some of these themes in the following paragraphs.

Family, marriage and parenthood

What is a family? The 1995 Church of England Report *Something to Celebrate*[4] found itself the subject of much criticism for its approach to questions of cohabitation, and its suggestion that the phrase 'living in sin' is not pastorally helpful. It was also criticized for its approach to the theology of the family. It is sad that by opening itself to criticism in its handling of these issues, the main purpose of the Report was obscured. This was to reflect on the enormous importance of family and community as offering us opportunities to give and receive from others. As the Report put it, 'Families are where we learn to love.'[5] The Report also reflected the considerable diversity of social arrangements which go under the name of 'family'. They force us to ask, 'What is a family?'

In an article which I wrote with Professor David Brown, we suggest that family can be best thought of as a 'covenant of care'.[6] The family, we argued, is a way of being which derives its meaning from the nature of God. By exploring our understanding of the nature of God, 'the Father, from whom his whole family . . . derives its name' (Eph. 3:14–15), we concluded that 'family' is a context for creativity in love, and that the task of parenthood within families is to provide 'authority for freedom, protection for growth, and revelation for understanding'. Family, marriage and the roles of parents and children are all intertwined.

---

[4] *Something to Celebrate: Valuing Families in Church and Society*; the report of a working party of the Board for Social Responsibility (Church House Publishing, 1995).

[5] *Ibid.*, p. 7.

[6] 'The Future of the Family', reprinted as ch. 6 in David Atkinson, *Pastoral Ethics* (Lynx, 1994).

In Proverbs, Wisdom places a high value on marriage and family life. We have seen that much of the teaching in the opening chapters is presented as from fathers to sons. In fact the word which the NIV translates as 'sons' (*bānîm*) often means 'children', and so does not exclude daughters. Although, as we have noted before, women generally receive less attention in Proverbs, this was partly no doubt due to the different status granted to women generally in Old Testament society. That is not necessarily to say that women had a *lower* status. On the one hand the practice of polygamy and concubinage seems to suggest this, though nowhere is polygamy commanded or commended in the Old Testament, and most of its examples are pretty disastrous. On the other hand, the laws of the Pentateuch in places display a very compassionate and protective dimension towards women (for example, the protection against male cruelty in the regulations concerned with a bill of divorcement in Dt. 24),[7] and Proverbs seems to delight in monogamy. By the time we reach the New Testament, we find that Jesus' attitude to women accords them a dignity which shocked and surprised even some of his followers (*cf. e.g.* Lk. 15:1–2; Jn. 4:9). And St Paul's classic charter of humanity in Galatians 3:28 – which could form the basic for an essential 'equal opportunities policy' in every aspect of life – affirms that in terms of spiritual status before God, there is no difference of gender or race or social starting-point; all are one in Christ Jesus.

Although in Proverbs there is more about men than about women, sometimes (*e.g.* chapter 31) it is women who are held up as shining examples of goodness.

We are told that a man is favoured if he finds a wife: 'He who finds a wife finds what is good and receives favour from the LORD' (18:22); 'Houses and wealth are inherited from parents, but a prudent wife is from the LORD'(19:14).

The wife is depicted as homemaker in 14:1, and in the idealized picture in 31:10ff. We recall from chapter 5 that it is in the context of the marriage covenant that sexual relationships belong and are celebrated (5:18ff.), and we cannot forget the lurid depictions of the adulteress, whose ways are always destruction and death.

These chapters of Proverbs illustrate that part of the gift God often gives to husbands and wives is the responsibility and joy of being parents, a significant dimension of whose task is to train children: 'Train a child in the way he should go, and when he is old he will not turn from it' (22:6). Good children, we learn, bring their parents joy, whereas foolish children bring grief: 'A wise son brings joy to his father, but a foolish son grief to his mother' (10:1); 'A wise

---

[7] Probably a regulation against the awful practice of loaning out one's wife for a time.

son brings joy to his father, but a foolish man despises his mother' (15:20).

In a most interesting and apt reference, we find that this extends across the generations. In a culture like ours, an ever-growing retired population is sometimes seen as a burden on the taxpayer and a drain on the resources of younger generations, leaving many grandparents to live in lonely isolation. But the picture we have in Proverbs is of a culture in which older people are honoured, and in which, rather than children being regarded as the pride of parents, parents are described as 'the pride of their children'. 'Children's children are a crown to the aged, and parents are the pride of their children' (17:6). That is a jolt to some contemporary western perspectives!

Proverbs also provides an illustration for the fifth commandment about the importance of the honour which children owe to parents: 'If a man curses his father or mother, his lamp will be snuffed out in pitch darkness' (20:20); 'He who robs his father and drives out his mother is a son who brings shame and disgrace' (19:26).

There is some self-interest here for children too, for they can expect to receive an inheritance from their parents, provided relationships are good: 'A good man leaves an inheritance for his children's children, but a sinner's wealth is stored up for the righteous' (13:22). However, 'He who brings trouble on his family will inherit only wind, and the fool will be servant to the wise' (11:29).

The significance of children is deepened in Jesus' attitude to them (cf. Mt. 18:2–4), and their response to parents is underlined in the New Testament, though Jesus himself, in his example and his teaching, shows that sometimes there is a higher duty to God, even above respect for family ties. St Paul makes clear the high value he places on children; in a marked reversal of some current Greek thought, he says that children are not there to look after parents, but parents to care for children (2 Cor. 12:14). And the pastoral letters emphasize the value of family life (cf. e.g. 1 Tim. 5.1ff.; 5:8; 5:14; 2 Tim. 1:5).

Proverbs also makes a point about the importance of good relationships within families, if they are to be places of mutual growth and nurture. We have already noticed the humorous comparison of the constantly quarrelsome wife with a dripping tap (19:13). It is better to live on the corner of a roof (21:9) or even in the desert (21:19) than to have to put up with that! On the other hand, 'A wife of noble character is her husband's crown, but a disgraceful wife is like decay in his bones' (12:4).

Diligence, creativity and hard work

The second selection of verses illustrating basic human needs includes those concerned with the world of work.

The need and opportunity for work were of course assumed in the Old Testament. Although some writers focus on work as a gift in which the worker expresses something of the creativity of God (Gn. 1 – 2; Ps. 104:23), others reflect how, in this fallen world, work has too often become toil and meaningless drudgery (Gn. 3:19; Ec. 2:19–23). We are faced in the Bible by both these positive and negative aspects to work, and the tension we constantly experience between them. The Bible does not, however, refer to dole queues, unemployment figures, reskilling, or youth training schemes. The work of industrial society is very different from the work in which the local extended family unit was also very largely an economic unit, and in which the worker could see and appreciate the end product of his labours. The *Communist Manifesto* commented 150 years ago:

> Owing to the extensive use of machinery and to division of labour, the work of the proletarians has lost all individual character and, consequently, all charm for the workman. He becomes an appendage of the machine, and it is only the most simple, the most monotonous, and most easily acquired knack that is required of him.

What would Karl Marx have made of the silicon chip, the robot, the Internet, and the computer imaging, which in western society at least are increasingly transforming the meaning of the word 'work'? Whereas earlier societies traded in beans and in cattle, and until recently we used to trade in money, now 'information' is the new currency, and data protection the new security nightmare.

Why is work important? Not because by working harder we will get richer; there is no simple equation between hard work and wealth. We work essentially because we have been given gifts of creativity to use in God's world. Work is our human activity which corresponds to the work of God in his providential care for the whole created order.[8]

---

[8] Karl Barth makes the point that we can think of the activity of God as a circle having a centre. The centre of God's activity is building his kingdom; the circumference is his providence which maintains the world in being for the kingdom to be built. Our human activity, he says, corresponds to God's. The centre is our service of the kingdom of God. The circumference for us – which corresponds to God's providence – is our work. *Cf.* Barth, *Church Dogmatics* III/4 (T. and T. Clark, 1961), ch. 55.

The world of Proverbs illustrates a society in which, if people did not work, they did not eat. So hard work is valued. 'The lazy man does not roast his game [because he doesn't have any game to roast!], but the diligent man prizes his possessions' (12:27). 'The labourer's appetite works for him; his hunger drives him on' (16:26). 'One who is slack in his work is brother to one who destroys' (18:9). 'Laziness brings on deep sleep, and the shiftless man goes hungry' (19:15).

But the value underlying much of the concern of Proverbs is the diligent attention needed to live in God's world, and conversely the folly of indolence. We recall how the sluggard received a pretty poor press in the opening chapters of Proverbs, and in fact was contrasted in chapter 6 rather unflatteringly with the hard-working ant. The same themes are found in these chapters. If you love sleep too much, you won't have food to live on (20:13). The sluggard is too lazy to feed himself (19:24), to plough his fields (20:4) or to do any work (21:25–26). In contrast to the profitable rewards which come the way of the diligent worker (21:5), the sluggard's rewards are a constant craving for more, which is never satisfied; and the end of that road is death (21:25–26).

One of the key themes which does link back without any difficulty into the twentieth-century world seems to be the irresponsibility of the sluggard. He would rather stay in bed than take responsibility for his life. He would rather stay dependent on the goodwill of others than seek to make something of his own life. He would rather stay safely in his indolence than take the risk of making relationships. With heavy, humorous sarcasm, the proverb recounts the sluggard saying, 'There is a lion outside!' as an excuse for inactivity, or even, 'I will be murdered in the streets!' as an excuse for not leaving his sofa (22:13). This is not saying anything about a dependency culture, or about those who would love to work but cannot find paid employment. Rather, it is reminding the readers that living in the way of wisdom is inevitably also the way of responsibility.

Health

Good health is another of Wisdom's concerns – another basic human need. But what is health? Health is one of those words which can mean a number of things. At one extreme, we could take as an example the approach of the World Health Organization, which seems to verge on the utopian: 'Health is a state of complete physical, mental and social well-being, not simply the absence of illness and disease.' At the other extreme, especially if we are managing tight budgets, we understand health strictly in physical terms as the absence of physical illness or disease.[9]

If our definition of health is to advocate an ideal pattern of life for individuals and for society, we will tend towards the former. If we are hospital managers, or those who are seeking to allocate all-too-limited healthcare resources, we will tend towards the latter. Most of us, of course, are somewhere between. But even so, there are ambiguities. In physical terms, health might refer to length of life, or to agility or strength or resistance to disease. Is a person more healthy when one part of him or her is working exceptionally well, or when all parts are reasonably in harmony? In mental-health terms, the definitions of mental health in the literature are very numerous.

Theologically, we need to reflect how, in the Old Testament, health is closely linked with shalom,[10] which as we have said means well-being at all levels of life and relationships. Shalom has an individual and a corporate dimension; it covers physical, emotional, relational and spiritual well-being. When the LORD brings peace, there is prosperity (Ps. 72:1–7), health (Is. 57:19), conciliation (Gn. 26:29) and contentedness (Gn. 15:15; Ps. 4:8). When the peace of the LORD is present, there are good relationships between nations and people (1 Ch. 12:17–18). God's shalom has a social aspect as well as an individual one (Je. 29:7).

We also need to remember the biblical concept of sin, and that ill health is seen as a symptom not usually of individual sins, but of the general fallenness of this world subject to decay and death. We need, too, to recall the biblical concept of restoration and salvation, in which God is making all things new.

In that context, a theology of health might regard the WHO definition as both too limited and too broad.[11] It is too limited because it does not link health at all to a person's spiritual life and relationship with God. It is also too limited because it concentrates on a person's 'state of well-being' and ignores the constant change in a person's life story and the story of his or her faith. But it is too broad in failing to recognize the inevitability of death, and in failing to see that suffering can itself be part of the strength to live healthily. Where it succeeds, however, is in recognizing the psychosomatic and social unity which is the human person, and the fact that all parts of us belong and grow in relation to each other.

This is the point at which a return to Proverbs is instructive. Long

---

[9] Cf. here A. Fergusson (ed.), *Health: The Strength to be Human* (IVP, 1993), including D. Atkinson, 'Towards a Theology of Health', reprinted in D. Atkinson, *Pastoral Ethics* (Lynx, 1994).

[10] Cf. the linking of these concepts in e.g. Is. 53:5 and Je. 8:15.

[11] Atkinson, 'Towards a Theology of Health', in Fergusson (ed.), op. cit., p. 176.

before medicine used the phrase 'psychosomatic illness', the writer of Proverbs said this: 'Do not be wise in your own eyes; fear the LORD and shun evil. This will bring health to your body and nourishment to your bones' (3:7–8). Here spiritual, moral, and physical aspects of health are brought together.

Proverbs also has quite a lot to say about concern for those who are downcast in spirit, and suffering the crippling effects of depression. Sometimes this is coupled with advice, which of course needs pastoral sensitivity. As we said before, Proverbs is not providing us with prescriptive commands to be obeyed in all circumstances, but rather with little vignettes which face us with the question of our reactions. 'Would this be the appropriate response to this person? Would it rather be better to see things like this?' To use a medical analogy: a doctor might say, 'Here is a prescription which I have found helpful in some cases like yours.' The task then is to try it out and see whether it helps us on our journey towards wholeness.

Here are some examples of possible diagnosis and possible response. 'An anxious heart weighs a man down, but a kind word cheers him up' (12:25). There is a poignant realism too: 'Even in laughter the heart may ache; and joy may end in grief' (14:13). Some forms of adversity are more bearable than others: 'A man's spirit sustains him in sickness, but a crushed spirit who can bear?' (18:14). And everyone has his or her own inner recesses of private grief or happiness where only God knows what is going on (14:10; 17:3; 21:2).

Other psychological advice includes these words: 'Hope deferred makes the heart sick, but a longing fulfilled is a tree of life' (13:12; 14:30); 'A heart at peace gives life to the body, but envy [perhaps meaning passionate as opposed to tranquil] rots the bones' (14:30).[12]

There are some Christian counsellors who seem to want to turn the book of Proverbs into a mental-health textbook. I believe we must be very wary of taking pithy 'gnomic' sayings, which are intended to make us think, as though they all enshrined principles which can be applied in all circumstances. Particularly in the area of counselling people who are anxious or depressed, Rule 1 is that everyone is different: the life story which has brought the person to this state of anxiety is entirely his or her own. And though, of course, there are general patterns in various emotional and mental

---

[12] Cf. also: 'Reckless words pierce like a sword, but the tongue of the wise brings healing' (12:18); 'A wicked messenger falls into trouble, but a trustworthy envoy brings healing' (13:17); 'The tongue that brings healing is a tree of life, but a deceitful tongue crushes the spirit' (15:4); 'A happy heart makes the face cheerful, but heartache crushes the spirit' (15:13); 'Pleasant words are a honeycomb, sweet to the soul and healing to the bones' (16:24); 'A cheerful heart is good medicine, but a crushed spirit dries up the bones' (17:22).

disturbances, there is more than usual need for pastoral sensitivity in seeking to offer help.

One well-known Christian counsellor seems to me to come dangerously near to overgeneralizing Proverbs in this respect when he says, quoting 4:20–22:

> The Bible teaches that a peace of mind which leads to longer, happier living comes from keeping God's commandments . . . A good conscience is one significant factor which leads to longevity and physical health . . . A close psychosomatic connection between one's behaviour before God and his physical condition is an established biblical principle.[13]

We can all think of people for whom this 'principle' is wonderfully true. It is also true that pastoral counselling may sometimes helpfully move over into spiritual direction. However, we can also think of biblical and other examples where suffering seems not to be linked to disobedience (see *e.g.* Jn. 9:3), and where young, godly people are none the less in ill health (*e.g.* Timothy, 1 Tim. 5:23). There is a tendency in some styles of Christian counselling to make the book of Proverbs into a Christian counsellor's handbook,[14] giving the impression that the sum total of counselling is directive confrontation and calling a person to moral responsibility. That may be the end of the story in some cases, but often there is a need to receive much of the love which casts out fear before we can dare to face the truth which sets us free.[15]

Security and safety

Another of the basic human needs about which Wisdom takes time to teach her pupils is the importance of security and safety. Sometimes the writers urge their readers to find a safe highway through life, frequently contrasting the safety and security of the righteous with the fragility of the ungodly. This is usually to encourage righteous living and the avoidance of wicked ways. And,

---

[13] Jay E. Adams, *Competent to Counsel* (Baker, 1970), p. 123.

[14] So Jay Adams, criticizing Rogerian methods: 'The system of counseling advocated in the Book of Proverbs is plainly nouthetic [Adams' word for counselling which involves confronting and warning the client with the demands of God expressed in Scripture]. Proverbs assumes the need for divine wisdom imparted (as in nouthetic counseling) by verbal means: by instruction, by reproof, by rebuke, by correction, and by applying God's commandments in order to change behaviour for one's benefit.' *Competent to Counsel*, p. 99.

[15] *Cf.* F. Bridger and D. Atkinson, *Counselling in Context* (HarperCollins, 1994), esp. ch. 10.

as we have said before, there is no necessary connection between good living and a sense of security. Godly people are not necessarily protected from burglars or road accidents. We can often feel insecure even though our outward circumstances may suggest otherwise. Sometimes this is through hurts rooted in childhood. Sometimes the circumstances of later life bring stresses too heavy to handle. We do not need to be in a war zone to realize that life can be fragile. A journey along a busy motorway can leave us with the same message. In fact, as we noticed in our reference earlier to Psalm 73, there are often times when godliness does not seem to bring much benefit: 'I envied the arrogant when I saw the prosperity of the wicked . . . Surely in vain I have kept my heart pure' (Ps. 73:3, 13).

In the New Testament, the first letter of Peter uses Proverbs 11:31 in its discussion of suffering. Sometimes suffering can be participating in the sufferings of Christ (1 Pet. 4:13). This can be a source of joy and strength, and should provoke us to commit ourselves even more faithfully to God our faithful creator (1 Pet. 4:19). For when God's judgment falls, those who do not obey the gospel will suffer even more. At this point the writer picks up the proverb, which originally discusses two sorts of people, and uses it as an illustration of judgment day: 'If the righteous receive their due on earth, how much more the ungodly and the sinner!' (Pr. 11:31; *cf.* 1 Pet. 4:18).

However, to return to Psalm 73: when the psalmist can see things from the perspective of eternity, he realizes that his real security is the 'refuge' of his God, who is 'the strength of my heart and my portion for ever' (26). Until that day dawns, however, he has to live in the faith expressed by the word 'yet' (or in the RSV 'Nevertheless'): 'Yet I am always with you' (23).

Faith does not take away all uncertainties. Faith does not make everything secure in a material or even an emotional sense. But faith is what God gives us to hold on to us in our uncertainties, and the confidence that he never lets go of our hand.

It is that faith, expressed as we have seen before in certain parts of Proverbs, through which we now read the 'gnomic' passages which speak of safety and security. Of course a sense of security is basic to our human well-being, as these proverbs show; they also constantly link the way of the righteous – those who are 'right with God' – with 'the way of the LORD'. So we learn that 'The fear of the LORD leads to life' (19:23), and, in contrast to the sluggard's path, which is blocked with thorns', 'the path of the upright is a highway' (15:19). It is important to escape trouble (12:13); indeed the righteous person finds he is rescued from trouble (11:8) and no harm befalls him (12:21). Such security is closely linked with being in the right with God (10:9). When the storm is over, and the wicked are swept away, those who are in the right with God stand firm: 'When the storm has swept by, the wicked are gone, but the righteous stand firm for ever' (10:25; cf. 10:29).[16]

To repeat what we have said before: security in the LORD is an affirmation of faith to live by, not a description of how life often feels.

Material sufficiency

Wisdom is concerned with human flourishing, with all that makes for health and security, with the good life, with shalom. This includes, therefore, the basic necessities of food, clothing, shelter and sufficient material wealth. We need to bear in mind what we have said frequently before, that these particular passages need to be read alongside other verses which very particularly stress the obligations of godly people towards the needs of the poor. When we read here that 'wealth brings many friends, but a poor man's friends desert him' (19:4), this looks like a commendation of wealth and a denigration of poverty. And in a sense it is. There are occasions when it is right to recognize that money can bring material well-being. It is also right to underline the powerlessness of poverty. But we cannot read this in the western world without also reflecting on the fact that many of the poor of the Third World are poor because their 'friends' in the rich West have deserted them. Some of their poverty comes from our injustice. The iniquities of Third World debt are largely to be laid at the door of First World greed.

Commenting in 1995 on recent changes in British society, Will Hutton of the *Guardian* writes in his best-selling *The State We're In* of 'the thirty, thirty, forty society':

> Society is dividing before our eyes, opening up new social fissures in the working population. The first 30 per cent are the *disadvantaged*. These include more than 4 million men who are out of work . . . altogether some 28 per cent of the adult working population are either unemployed or economically inactive . . . The second 30 per cent are made of the *marginalised* and the *insecure* . . . People in this category work at jobs that are insecure, poorly protected and carry few benefits . . . [plus] the growing army of part-timers and casual workers . . . Just under 30 per cent

[16] *Cf.* also: 'The righteous will never be uprooted, but the wicked will not remain in the land' (10:30); 'A man cannot be established through wickedness, but the righteous cannot be uprooted' (12:3); 'Wicked men are overthrown and are no more, but the house of the righteous stands firm' (12:7); 'A fool's talk brings a rod to his back, but the lips of the wise protect them' (14:3); 'The house of the wicked will be destroyed, but the tent of the upright will flourish' (14:11); 'When calamity comes, the wicked are brought down, but even in death the righteous have a refuge' (14:32).

of the labour force by these definitions are insecure and margin-
alised . . . The last category is that of the *privileged* – the just over
40 per cent whose market power has increased since 1979 . . . The
fact that more than half the people in Britain who are eligible to
work are either living on poverty incomes or in conditions of
permanent stress and insecurity has had dreadful effects on the
wider society.[17]

The proverbs we look at in this section need to be read in this
light. They are not general principles saying, 'This is true', but
pointed word pictures which ask us: 'Is this true of you? If so, how
should you then live?'

Food

Numerous proverbs celebrate the provision of food as one of life's
needs and one of God's gifts. Here is a selection: 'The LORD does
not let the righteous go hungry but he thwarts the craving of the
wicked' (10:3). 'Better to be a nobody and yet have a servant than
pretend to be somebody and have no food' (12:9). 'The righteous eat
to their heart's content, but the stomach of the wicked goes hungry'
(13:25). 'Where there are no oxen, the manger is empty, but from the
strength of an ox comes an abundant harvest' (14:4).

The recognition that food is a gift from God (10:3) is used as an
incentive for generosity to those who are hungry. If even our enemy
is hungry, we should feed him; if he is thirsty, we should give him
drink (25:21, quoted in Rom. 12:20).

As we saw earlier in Proverbs 3, there is a ready movement of
thought from the call to honour the LORD (9), to the provision of
barns and vats (10), to the obligation of generosity (27). God's
provision for us commits us to providing for others. We cannot pray
'Give us today our daily bread' without at the same time taking steps
to provide bread for those who are without.

Satisfaction

A number of proverbs speak of 'satisfaction' as a result of diligent
and godly living. Whereas 'the sluggard craves and gets nothing',
'the desires of the diligent are fully satisfied' (13:4). Similarly, a
'longing fulfilled is sweet to the soul' (13:19), and a 'cheerful heart
has a continual feast' (15:15). These proverbs in fact contrast the
diligent with the sluggard, the righteous person with the fool, the
cheerful person with the wretched. Such a contrast again provokes

[17] Will Hutton, *The State We're In* (Jonathan Cape, 1995), pp. 105ff.

the question how we are to respond to the different status of people around us, in particular to those who are oppressed and whose days are wretched, who have nothing and no-one to cheer their heart.

Sufficient wealth

Proverbs has quite a lot to say about wealth. Usually 'wealth' or 'riches' is contrasted with 'poverty', and so does not mean extravagance, but sufficiency. Wealth is the result of human labour (10:16; 13:11), of 'diligent hands' (10:4), and of 'the blessing of the LORD' (10:22; *cf.* 13:21). It can be used to make friends (14:20) or to dominate the poor (18:23). Ill-gotten treasures are of no ultimate value for life (10:2). There is a temptation to pretend to be rich when you have nothing, or to be poor in order to hide great wealth (13:7). Sufficient wealth can bring security (10:15; 18:11), and can provide an inheritance for a person's children (13:22). The provision of sufficiency is linked to the often repeated formula that generosity towards others has the effect of bringing in more to oneself: 'One man gives freely, yet gains even more; another withholds unduly, but comes to poverty' (11:24). There are cautions, however, in the misuse of money and wealth. Riches can be a snare (13:8). To gather money little by little makes it grow (13:11).

Poverty, we are reminded again and again, brings shame; it isolates; it alienates: 'He who ignores discipline comes to poverty and shame, but whoever heeds correction is honoured' (13:18). 'The poor are shunned even by their neighbours, but the rich have many friends' (14:20). 'All hard work brings a profit, but mere talk leads only to poverty' (14:23). As we underlined earlier: 'Wealth brings many friends, but a poor man's friends desert him' (19:4).

It is perhaps as well, as we close this section, to remind ourselves again that we cannot use Proverbs to boost the sort of 'prosperity gospel' which some televangelists (especially in the USA) seem to offer. Come to God, preferably with your cheque book ready, and all your problems will be over. In some respects many of the proverbs on their own *can* be taken as a sort of success manual, and indeed have been so taken by the prosperity gospellers. But, as we have said before, we need to see the proverbs partly as pertinent pictures to shake us and ask us to think again, and partly as an aspect of the wider wisdom tradition in which suffering, pain and uncertainty also have a role in the life of faith. The book of Job, for example, refuses to allow us to follow the prosperity-gospel route.[18] But Proverbs, as we saw earlier in this chapter, also has a realistic

[18] *Cf.* David Atkinson, *The Message of Job* (IVP, 1991).

understanding of the many uncertainties and perplexities of faith which 'make the heart sad'.[19]

The importance of appropriate speech

In one way or another, the writers of Proverbs have quite a lot to say about the tongue. As the letter of James in the New Testament underlines, how we speak is a pretty good indication of our character. The tongue is like a very small rudder which can set the direction for a very large ship, even when the winds outside are strong (Jas. 3:4ff.). The tongue can speak praises to God. The same tongue can speak curses to other people (Jas. 3:9ff.). Though a small part of the body, its effects are very large. 'Consider what a great forest is set on fire by a small spark' (Jas. 3:5). In writing like this, James is very close to the style of many proverbs. Some of them are concerned at the ill effects of gossiping. Some are on the need to avoid quarrelling and dissension. Some are on the power of anger, and some are on the value of speaking the truth. We will explore these in turn.

Gossips

It is interesting how unfriendly a press gossips get in the New Testament, and how little that fact is noticed. We are often too concerned about other themes in Romans 1, for example, to notice that 'gossips' (or perhaps 'whisperers') feature in the list of those against whom God's judgment is expressed (Rom. 1:29). Cranfield notes that the terms 'denote people who go about to destroy others' reputation by misrepresentation'.[20] Similarly, 'slanderers' are on Paul's list of those whose lives do not match up to the kingdom of God (1 Cor. 6:9). It is interesting that in Paul's day, as in ours, the Christian church was not immune from whisperers. Some people simply cannot keep confidences. Some share personal information about others 'just for your prayers'. Some deliberately make a point of criticizing other's behaviour and reputation. There is a pernicious power in such whispering, and indeed, perhaps it is out of a desire for the power it brings that people give way to it so much. But such behaviour comes between friends, creates disorder, and sows discord. Proverbs said as much centuries ago: 'A perverse man stirs

---

[19] An interesting comment on the work of one particular popular American preacher, Robert Schuller, of the Crystal Cathedral in California, is found in Dennis Voskuil, *Mountains into Goldmines: Robert Schuller and the Gospel of Success* (Eerdmans, 1983).

[20] C. E. B. Cranfield, *Romans: A Shorter Commentary* (T. & T. Clark, 1985), p. 37.

up dissension, and a gossip separates close friends' (16:28); 'A gossip betrays a confidence; so avoid a man who talks too much' (20:19).

Proverbs takes this further to suggest that it is better even to be poor than to be a person of perverse speech (19:1). A wise person will not plot against others: 'He who winks with his eye is plotting perversity; he who purses his lips is bent on evil' (16:30).

Quarrels

The wise writer of Proverbs regards it as folly to stir up dissension in the community. Quarrelling very soon turns into sin. It disrupts relationships and is always destructive. So a wise person will avoid malice and quarrels. 'He who loves a quarrel loves sin; he who builds a high gate invites destruction' (17:19). 'A fool's lips bring him strife, and his mouth invites a beating. A fool's mouth is his undoing, and his lips are a snare to his soul. The words of a gossip are like choice morsels; they go down to a man's inmost parts' (18:6–8).[21] 'Drive out the mocker, and out goes strife; quarrels and insults are ended' (22:10).

Anger

If quarrelling is always destructive, anger is not always so. It is possible to express anger appropriately; indeed, in the face of injustice or the defamation of holy things, anger is the appropriate reaction. Jesus in the temple took a whip in his hands to drive out the money-changers who were plying their trade in the temple court. He 'snorted with indignation' (literally; NIV, 'he was deeply moved'; Jn. 11:33) in front of the grave of Lazarus at the intrusion of death into the world, to which he came to bring resurrection and life (Jn. 11:25). In his fine book *The Gospel of Anger*,[22] Alistair Campbell comments on the way anger can be a positive human emotion:

> Anger may be denied, but it cannot be eliminated from human life, and the more we refuse to face up to it the more it will undermine the possibilities of true Christian love through a cloying 'niceness' or an ill-concealed resentment. In considering how we deal with anger pastorally, so that it becomes not an enemy of love, but part of the gospel of love, we must look again at the kinds of situations in which it is most readily aroused, and then consider what a *loving* anger might achieve in overcoming both enmity and apathy.[23]

---

[21] *Cf.* 'A wicked man listens to evil lips; a liar pays attention to a malicious tongue' (17:4); 'He who guards his mouth and his tongue keeps himself from calamity' (21:23).

[22] Alistair V. Campbell, *The Gospel of Anger* (SPCK, 1986).

[23] *Ibid.*, p. 94 (emphasis in original).

Campbell then considers situations of vulnerability, loss and oppression, in which 'loving anger' may be appropriate. However, Campbell is also quick to notice the very close connection between inappropriate anger and destructiveness. He argues that the task which faces us,

> . . . if the Christian commitment to compassion and to justice is to be honoured in the way we act towards others, as individuals and nations, is to sever the link between anger and destructiveness and to find ways in which people's powerful reactions to life's dangers around them may be put to the service of human wholeness.[24]

This is perhaps the point underlying the very close link between anger and sin in Ephesians 4:26, quoting Psalm 4:4: 'In your anger do not sin.' The same tension of understanding, even ambiguity, in the way it speaks of anger, is found in Proverbs. A wise person will control his temper, turn away wrath, and take care with his tongue: 'A quick-tempered man does foolish things, and a crafty man is hated' (14:17). 'A patient man has great understanding, but a quick-tempered man displays folly' (14:29). 'A gentle answer turns away wrath, but a harsh word stirs up anger' (15:1). 'A hot-tempered man stirs up dissension, but a patient man calms a quarrel' (15:18).[25]

Truth

Proverbs 15 includes many wise sayings on the importance of how we speak. We have already noticed that 'A gentle answer turns away wrath' (1). But we also learn that 'The tongue of the wise commends knowledge' (2), 'The tongue that brings healing is a tree of life' (4),

---

[24] *Ibid.*, p. 31.

[25] *Cf.* also: 'A man of knowledge uses words with restraint, and a man of understanding is even-tempered. Even a fool is thought wise if he keeps silent, and discerning if he holds his tongue' (17:27–28); 'Casting the lot settles disputes and keeps strong opponents apart. An offended brother is more unyielding than a fortified city, and disputes are like the barred gates of a citadel. From the fruit of his mouth a man's stomach is filled; with the harvest from his lips he is satisfied. The tongue has the power of life and death, and those who love it will eat its fruit' (18:18–21); 'Better a poor man whose walk is blameless than a fool whose lips are perverse' (19:1); 'It is to a man's honour to avoid strife, but every fool is quick to quarrel' (20:3). 'A hot-tempered man must pay the penalty; if you rescue him, you will have to do it again' (19:19). Even the power of a bribe (elsewhere condemned) is noted as a means of pacifying an angry judge: 'A gift given in secret soothes anger, and a bribe concealed in the cloak pacifies great wrath' (21:14). Chapters 16 and 17 have some vivid imagery to make the same point: 'Better a patient man than a warrior, a man who controls his temper than one who takes a city' (16:32); 'Better a dry crust with peace and quiet than a house full of feasting, with strife' (17:1); 'Starting a quarrel is like breaching a dam; so drop the matter before a dispute breaks out' (17:14).

and 'The lips of the wise spread knowledge' (7). The chapter then interestingly refers to appropriate patterns of using our speech in prayer. The 'prayer of the upright pleases' God (8); 'The LORD hears the prayer of the righteous' (29).

It is as if the writer wants us to make a connection like this: 'Take great care how you speak and what you say: all you say is heard by the LORD.' Perhaps Wisdom is suggesting that all our speech should be a prayer. Certainly, elsewhere, Wisdom indicates the importance of avoiding lies and speaking truth, and perhaps that is nowhere more important than before God. We could almost define prayer as the openness before God which avoids lies – allowing him to see and be part of all of us just as we are, with our hurts and pains and as yet unredeemed sinfulness – and which seeks to be brought more into line with the truth which sets free (cf. Jn. 8:32). Here is Proverbs: 'A false witness will not go unpunished, and he who pours out lies will not go free' (19:5, 9); 'A fortune made by a lying tongue is a fleeting vapour and a deadly snare' (21:6). Conversely, 'Gold there is, and rubies in abundance, but lips that speak knowledge [perhaps, even, "lips of truth"] are a rare jewel' (20:15).

The king's glory and the national honour

From values undergirding personal, family and community life, we now turn to the national scene. It is important to the wise writers that the city be in good heart and good health. As the prophet Jeremiah later reminded the exiles, the people should pray even for the city of Babylon: 'If it prospers, you too will prosper' (Je. 29:7).

The wise set high value on joy in the city: 'When the righteous prosper, the city rejoices; when the wicked perish, there are shouts of joy. Through the blessing of the upright a city is exalted, but by the mouth of the wicked it is destroyed' (11:10–11).

In such a context, it is also important that the king should observe the ways of wisdom, and that his court also should uphold wisdom's values. The king's security is linked to love and faithfulness (20:28). His well-being is linked to the well-being of his subjects and his court (14:28; 14:35). And it depends on his relationship with the LORD: The king's heart is in the hand of the LORD; he directs it like a watercourse wherever he pleases' (21:1).[26]

Clearly it is one of the duties of the king to be concerned for the

---

[26] Chapter 16 has a concentrated short paragraph on the king's values: 'The lips of a king speak as an oracle, and his mouth should not betray justice . . . Kings detest wrongdoing, for a throne is established through righteousness. Kings take pleasure in honest lips; they value a man who speaks the truth. A king's wrath is a messenger of death, but a wise man will appease it. When a king's face brightens, it means life; his favour is like a rain cloud in spring' (16:10–15).

welfare of his people, and so adjudicate between good and evil. He can show rage like a lion, or tenderness 'like dew on the grass' (19:12). It is not worth angering the king (20:2)! A wise king is known for his winnowing out of all evil, so that good can flourish (20:8, 26).

At the heart of the kingdom is the need for godly guidance. As a later writer put it, 'Where there is no vision, the people perish' (29:18, AV). Or, as in these chapters, 'For lack of guidance a nation falls, but many advisers make victory sure' (11:14). How important that those in ruling authority have a clear vision for their role and responsibilities under God, and are open to the advice which stems from true Wisdom!

It is interesting to place these paragraphs against the picture of a godly king drawn in idealized terms in Psalm 72. The king's rule is one of righteousness and justice (1–3) but, in that, he is subject to God's justice (1). Behind the earthly king is the kingly reign of God. The godly king will defend the cause of the poor, deliver the needy and crush the oppressor (4). The fruits of his godly leadership will be fertility and peace (6–7). Only after the king's righteousness has been celebrated is there any reference to the king's power (8–11). He is on the side of the poor and the needy (12–13), and sets a high value on every person's life (14). The psalmist is then taken up in prayer for the well-being of such a king (15–17). This king reflects the picture of the kingdom under David and Solomon at its most glorious, and the hopes of the people at their most faithful. These thoughts are not far from the hopes of the prophets who looked forward to the coming messianic king, of whose government and peace there would be no end, and whose calling is to establish and uphold the throne of David in justice and righteousness (Is. 9:7). Part of the function of the king is to establish the kingdom of shalom.

Animal welfare

We have noticed several times the importance the writers place on animal life, and the use of animals of different sorts to illustrate lessons which the readers should heed. Tucked away in Proverbs 12 is a little verse which we do well to notice. It knocks on the head the all-too-prevalent assumption that the people of the Old Testament understood the creation mandate in Genesis 1 to legitimize exploitation of the animal kingdom for human gain. On the contrary, 'A righteous man cares for the needs of his animal', even though 'the kindest acts of the wicked are cruel' (12:10).

Life, freedom and hope

We bring this chapter to a conclusion with a brief glance at the way Wisdom celebrates life and freedom, and (in the next section) with a recapitulation of the ways in which her pupils can grow in understanding.

Wisdom's celebration of life is underlined by various proverbs in these chapters. Again and again, 'righteousness' and 'life' are linked together. By 'righteousness' Proverbs means 'being right with God'. 'Life' sometimes means the life of physical organs, and sometimes the life-giving breath of the whole person in every dimension of his or her being. To be fully alive is to be right with the God who gives life. One proverb which links these two concepts is 10:16: 'The wages of the righteous bring them life, but the income of the wicked brings them punishment.'[27]

In many proverbs, we discover that the path of life is marked by careful talk, obedience and the way of wisdom. Thus, 'the mouth of the righteous is a fountain of life, but violence overwhelms the mouth of the wicked' (10:11); 'He who obeys instructions guards his life, but he who is contemptuous of his ways will die' (19:16); 'He who guards his lips guards his life, but he who speaks rashly will come to ruin' (13:3); 'The teaching of the wise is a fountain of life, turning a man from the snares of death' (13:14). The life of the righteous is also described as a life of freedom. For example: 'The righteousness of the upright delivers them, but the unfaithful are trapped by evil desires' (11:6).[28] And long life is particularly valued: 'The fear of the LORD adds length to life, but the years of the wicked are cut short' (10:27).[29] Wisdom wants her disciples to be delivered from death and from the judgment of 'the day of wrath' (e.g. 10:2; 11:4).[30]

A less frequent but no less important value is hope: 'When a wicked man dies, his hope perishes; all he expected from his power comes to nothing' (11:7). Is the implication that the hope of the righteous

---

[27] Cf. 'He who heeds discipline shows the way to life, but whoever ignores correction leads others astray' (10:17); 'The truly righteous man attains life, but he who pursues evil goes to his death' (11:19); 'The fruit of the righteous is a tree of life, and he who wins souls is wise' (11:30); 'In the way of righteousness there is life, along that path is immortality' (12:28).

[28] Cf. 'Be sure of this: The wicked will not go unpunished, but those who are righteous will go free' (11:21).

[29] Cf. 'The light of the righteous shines brightly, but the lamp of the wicked is snuffed out' (13:9); 'The highway of the upright avoids evil; he who guards his way guards his life' (16:17).

[30] 'A truthful witness saves lives, but a false witness is deceitful' (14:25); 'The path of life leads upward for the wise to keep him from going down to the grave' (15:24); 'There is a way that seems right to a man, but in the end it leads to death' (14:12; 16:25).

endures? Much of Proverbs is written with an eye to the future: 'The prospect of the righteous is joy' (10:28). But much of the future is hidden, even to the eye of faith. Ultimately the future is in God's hands. 'The horse is made ready for the day of battle, but victory rests with the LORD' (21:31). 'In his heart a man plans his course, but the LORD determines his steps' (16:9). That is why the righteous man must wait on the LORD, who corrects the man's own plans. True hope must be hope in the LORD: 'Do not say, "I'll pay you back for this wrong!" Wait for the LORD, and he will deliver you' (20:22).

Knowledge and understanding

Underlying all Wisdom's teaching is the supreme practical value of knowledge and understanding. Again and again the student is told to get wisdom, and to develop a willingness to learn.

Wisdom often employs the metaphor of the good life as a journey, a straight way: 'The righteousness of the blameless makes a straight way for them, but the wicked are brought down by their own wickedness' (11:5).[31] So the wise pupil, in following this way, must take several positive steps. First, the learner in the school of Wisdom must avoid folly. 'Understanding is a fountain of life to those who have it, but folly brings punishment to fools' (16:22).[32] He needs secondly to avoid pride: 'Pride goes before destruction, a haughty spirit before a fall' (16:18).[33] Thirdly, he needs to grow in discernment: 'Wisdom is found on the lips of the discerning, but a rod is for the back of him who lacks judgment' (10:13).[34] Fourthly, he must grow in prudence and discernment: 'A prudent man keeps his knowledge to himself, but the heart of fools blurts out folly' (12:23).[35] Finally, he must love knowledge: 'Whoever loves discipline loves knowledge, but he who hates correction is stupid' (12:1); 'The

[31] Cf. 'The man of integrity walks securely, but he who takes crooked paths will be found out' (10:9); 'Folly delights a man who lacks judgment, but a man of understanding keeps a straight course' (15:21); 'A man who strays from the path of understanding comes to rest in the company of the dead' (21:16).

[32] Cf. 'To have a fool for a son brings grief; there is no joy for the father of a fool' (17:21); 'A foolish son brings grief to his father and bitterness to the one who bore him' (17:25); 'A man's folly ruins his life, yet his heart rages against the LORD' (19:3).

[33] Cf. 'Better to be lowly in spirit and among the oppressed than to share plunder with the proud' (16:19); 'Before his downfall a man's heart is proud, but humility comes before honour' (18:12); 'Haughty eyes and a proud heart, the lamp of the wicked, are sin!' (21:4); 'The proud and arrogant man – "Mocker" is his name; he behaves with overweening pride' (21:24).

[34] Cf. 'A rebuke impresses a man of discernment more than a hundred lashes a fool' (17:10).

[35] Cf. 'Like a gold ring in a pig's snout is a beautiful woman who shows no discretion' (11:22). 'A prudent man sees danger and takes refuge, but the simple keep going and suffer for it' (22:3).

eyes of the LORD keep watch over knowledge, but he frustrates the words of the unfaithful' (22:12).[36]

By contrast with the prudent person's growth in knowledge, the fool never seems to learn. In a verse whose first line is picked up in the second letter of Peter (2:22) to depict the hollow promises of false teachers, and the fact that they are worse off at the end than at the beginning, Proverbs uses the illustration of a dog: 'As a dog returns to its vomit, so a fool repeats his folly' (26:11).

The way of Wisdom, though, includes discretion, understanding, careful speech, humility and forethought: 'When words are many, sin is not absent, but he who holds his tongue is wise' (10:19); 'When pride comes, then comes disgrace, but with humility comes wisdom' (11:2).[37]

Here, then, are the benefits of Wisdom's way: 'How much better to get wisdom than gold, to choose understanding rather than silver!' (16:16); 'The wise in heart are called discerning, and pleasant words promote instruction' (16:21).[38] The wise pupil is one who shows a willingness to learn and to take advice: 'The way of a fool

---

[36] Cf. 'The mocker seeks wisdom and finds none, but knowledge comes easily to the discerning' (14:6); 'Stay away from a foolish man, for you will not find knowledge on his lips' (14:7); 'The simple inherit folly, but the prudent are crowned with knowledge' (14:18); 'The tongue of the wise commends knowledge, but the mouth of the fool gushes folly' (15:2); 'When a mocker is punished, the simple gain wisdom; when a wise man is instructed, he gets knowledge' (21:11). The wise pupil will not only acquire wisdom, but will store up knowledge: 'Wise men store up knowledge, but the mouth of a fool invites ruin' (10:14); 'Every prudent man acts out of knowledge, but a fool exposes his folly' (13:16); 'The lips of the wise spread knowledge; not so the heart of fools' (15:7); 'The discerning heart seeks knowledge, but the mouth of a fool feeds on folly' (15:14); 'The heart of the discerning acquires knowledge; the ears of the wise seek it out' (18:15); 'It is not good to have zeal without knowledge, nor to be hasty and miss the way' (19:2); 'Flog a mocker and the simple will learn prudence; rebuke a discerning man, and he will gain knowledge' (19:25).

[37] Cf. 'A fool finds pleasure in evil conduct, but a man of understanding delights in wisdom' (10:23); 'The mouth of the righteous brings forth wisdom, but a perverse tongue will be cut out' (10:31); 'A man is praised according to his wisdom, but men with warped minds are despised' (12:8); 'A fool shows his annoyance at once, but a prudent man overlooks an insult' (12:16); 'A wise son heeds his father's instruction, but a mocker does not listen to rebuke' (13:1); 'He who walks with the wise grows wise, but a companion of fools suffers harm' (13:20); 'A simple man believes anything, but a prudent man gives thought to his steps' (14:15); 'A fool spurns his father's discipline, but whoever heeds correction shows prudence' (15:5); 'A fool finds no pleasure in understanding but delights in airing his own opinions' (18:2); 'The words of a man's mouth are deep waters, but the fountain of wisdom is a bubbling brook' (18:4).

[38] Cf. 'A wise servant will rule over a disgraceful son, and will share the inheritance as one of the brothers' (17:2); 'A discerning man keeps wisdom in view, but a fool's eyes wander to the ends of the earth' (17:24); 'It is a trap for a man to dedicate something rashly and only later to consider his vows' (20:25); 'In the house of the wise are stores of choice food and oil, but a foolish man devours all he has' (21:20); 'A

seems right to him, but a wise man listens to advice' (12:15); 'Stop listening to instruction, my son, and you will stray from the words of knowledge' (19:27).[39]

These, then, are some of the ways in which the wise guided their pupils and parents guided their children. It is worth balancing this with the New Testament perception (which endorses much of what Proverbs also says) that children often have an incisive and innocent perception that cuts through adult views, and can sometimes get to truth which is hidden to adults' cluttered minds. Was this what Jesus was doing when he called a little child and had him stand among them (Mt. 18:2)?

In general these core values in Wisdom's character, which we have explored in this and in our previous section, can be translated into the different sorts of respect that human beings are encouraged to show towards God, their world and their neighbours if their lives are to flourish.

We began by noting the stress on the fear of the LORD, the reverent obedience due to God alone. We noticed the way Wisdom sees life as a journey, and reminds us of the proper use of time. We have read of respect for authority, within the nation and within the family structure. Wisdom's teachers refer to respect for one's own and for another's life and health. The importance of faithfulness in relationships is stressed; so is the value of material sufficiency and of one's own property, as well as the obligation to meet the needs of the poor. Wisdom teaches the importance of truthfulness. And above all it teaches the need to love enough not to be jealous, and the importance of the social expression of love, which is justice. Other values are there, too, but these seem to be the core.

They are by no means the same as current political values, which are often driven by economic factors or the assumption that to tighten up on structural and institutional issues such as law and order will restore the possibilities of more personal qualities such as friendship, community and belonging. Life, Wisdom will teach us, is defined not by material values, but in the light of the fear of the LORD. Community is achieved not by seeking what we can get, but

---

wicked man puts up a bold front, but an upright man gives thought to his ways' (21:29); 'The purposes of a man's heart are deep waters, but a man of understanding draws them out' (20:5).

[39] Cf. 'Pride only breeds quarrels, but wisdom is found in those who take advice' (13:10); 'He who scorns instruction will pay for it, but he who respects a command is rewarded' (13:13); 'Plans fail for lack of counsel, but with many advisers they succeed' (15:22); 'Whoever gives heed to instruction prospers, and blessed is he who trusts in the LORD' (16:20); 'He who answers before listening – that is his folly and his shame' (18:13); 'Listen to advice and accept instruction, and in the end you will be wise' (19:20); 'Make plans by seeking advice; if you wage war, obtain guidance' (20:18).

rather by expressing justice, love, compassion and a strong obligation to share what we have with those who are less advantaged than we are. Love to God and love to neighbour seem to be the sum of it, coupled with that expression of love which seeks for justice in all human affairs.

Another way of expressing this may be perceived in this treatment of the Ten Commandments in the 1980 *Alternative Service Book* of the Church of England:

Our Lord Jesus Christ said, If you love me, keep my commandments; happy are those who hear the word of God and keep it. Hear then these commandments which God has given to his people, and take them to heart.

I am the Lord your God: you shall have no other gods but me. You shall love the Lord your God with all your heart, with all your soul, with all your mind, and with all your strength.
> Amen. Lord, have mercy.

You shall not make for yourself any idol. God is spirit, and those who worship him must worship in spirit and in truth.
> Amen. Lord, have mercy.

You shall not dishonour the name of the Lord your God. You shall worship him with awe and reverence.
> Amen. Lord, have mercy.

Remember the Lord's day and keep it holy. Christ is risen from the dead: set your minds on things that are above, not on things that are on the earth.
> Amen. Lord, have mercy.

Honour your father and mother. Live as servants of God; honour all people; love the brotherhood.
> Amen. Lord, have mercy.

You shall not commit murder. Be reconciled to your brother; overcome evil with good.
> Amen. Lord, have mercy.

You shall not commit adultery. Know that your body is a temple of the Holy Spirit.
> Amen. Lord, have mercy.

You shall not steal. Be honest in all that you do and care for those in need.
> Amen. Lord, have mercy.

You shall not be a false witness.
Let everyone speak the truth.

> Amen. Lord, have mercy.

You shall not covet anything which belongs to your neighbour.
Remember the words of the Lord Jesus: It is more blessed to give
than to receive. Love your neighbour as yourself, for love is the
fulfilling of the law.

> Amen. Lord, have mercy.

Part 6
Wisdom's values:
The words of the wise

Sayings of the wise (22:17 – 24:22; 24:23–34)

We spent some time in Parts 1 and 2 looking at the first nine chapters of Proverbs, with their portrait of Wisdom, and the sections of fatherly instructions offered by parents to their young people. In Parts 4 and 5 we have been trying to uncover some of Wisdom's values: both the foundational values of love, justice and the fear of the LORD, and the more practical values associated with family, marriage, health, security and the use of the tongue. That concludes our discussion of the major section of the book of Proverbs which is collected together under the name of Solomon (1:1). A little later on we are offered some 'more proverbs of Solomon' (25:1), this time 'copied by the men of Hezekiah king of Judah'. Interspersed between the two collections which bear Solomon's name, there are two much shorter sections which the text introduces as 'sayings of the wise' (22:17; 24:23). The first of these sections itself falls into two parts, 22:17 – 23:14 and 23:15 – 24:22. We will look at them in turn.

Back in Wisdom's school (22:17 – 23:14)

It has often been noted by scholars how similar this section is to the Egyptian collection of proverbs, the *Wisdom of Amenemope*. That work has thirty chapters (*cf.* the reference to 'thirty sayings' in Pr. 22:20), which also offer instructions against exploiting the poor (*cf.* 22:22–23), about how to behave when you sit down to dinner with the king (*cf.* 23:1–3), against relying too much on riches (*cf.* 23:4–5), and about not moving ancient boundary stones (*cf.* 22:28; 23:10). Some scholars think that the wise men whose words we have in this section of Proverbs may well have borrowed material from this ancient Egyptian writing of about 1000 BC. Others are not so sure. But even if there is some borrowing, the 'wise' have deliberately pressed their material into the framework of a faith in the covenant Lord who will take up the cause of the poor (22:23), and is the defender (gō'ēl) of the fatherless (23:11; cf. Dt. 10:18).

The section starts with an author's introduction, which comments on the right use of proverbs. Once again we seem to be back in a school where study is taken seriously. There are strong reminders here of the teacher imparting instructions in the first nine chapters of Proverbs. We, the readers, are addressed again as 'my son'; we hear the teacher calling us to 'give attention'. This is all reminiscent of those opening themes.

The introduction (22:17–21) is similar to that in the prologue to the *Instruction of Amenemope*. The teacher is calling his pupils to attention (17) and reminding them of the benefits of doing so (18). Such an exercise is related to developing trust in Yahweh (19).

> *Pay attention and listen to the sayings of the wise;*
> *apply your heart to what I teach,*
> ¹⁸*for it is pleasing when you keep them in your heart*
> *and have all of them ready on your lips.*
> ¹⁹*So that your trust may be in the* LORD,
> *I teach you today, even you.*
> ²⁰*Have I not written thirty sayings for you,*
> *sayings of counsel and knowledge,*
> ²¹*teaching you true and reliable words,*
> *so that you can give sound answers*
> *to him who sent you?*

As learners in this school, we are to concentrate on study. If we do so, trust in the LORD will be deepened, and we will be better equipped to give sound advice to those who come to us for help. It is worth remarking, as we have done before, on the words the writer uses: verbs such as *Pay attention, listen, apply, keep them, have . . . them ready*; nouns such as *heart* and *lips*. Hubbard refers to 'the student's total engagement in the learning process'.[1] Wisdom demands my soul, my life, my all.

> *Do not exploit the poor because they are poor*
> *and do not crush the needy in court,*
> ²³*for the* LORD *will take up their case*
> *and will plunder those who plunder them.*
> ²⁴*Do not make friends with a hot-tempered man,*
> *do not associate with one easily angered,*

---

[1] Hubbard, p. 352.

> ²⁵*or you may learn his ways*
> *and get yourself ensnared.*
> ²⁶*Do not be a man who strikes hands in pledge*
> *or puts up security for debts;*
> ²⁷*if you lack the means to pay,*
> *your very bed will be snatched from under you.*

The set of sayings continues by expressing concern for the poor and disadvantaged, and the need to avoid bad company (22:22–25). *Exploit* and *crush* are strong verbs emphasizing the evil of injustice towards *the poor*. *The LORD will take up their case.* As elsewhere in the Old Testament, here we find the LORD on the side of the poor, the oppressed, the disadvantaged, the outcast and the stranger. Here is a call paralleled by the prophet Amos: 'Let justice roll on like a river, righteousness like a never-failing stream!' (5:24). The teacher in this school is reminding his pupils to be equally alert to the administration of justice in the court.

Leaders should be able to control their temper (22:24–25). These verses indicate the damage that anger can do. So we are urged to avoid friendship with those who are habitually *hot-tempered.* (A *hot-tempered man* means literally an 'owner of anger', someone for whom anger is a way of life.) To associate too closely with people like that can entrap us in a similarly damaging attitude.

Verses 26 and 27 warn us against incautious use of money in hasty pledges. And verse 28 safeguards the rights of the disadvantaged by securing land boundaries within which they should be safe. Unfortunately the land of the poor was often commandeered by the rich; this ruling was to safeguard their well-being. As we discussed earlier, in Part 4, the 'landmark' was essential to the sense of security in each family household. It reminded the people of God's gift of land. The Deuteronomic law made this quite explicit: 'Do not move your neighbour's boundary stone set up by your predecessors in the inheritance you receive in the land the LORD your God is giving you to possess' (Dt. 19:14).

Next comes a brief comment on the value of craftsmanship, and in praise of good business: 'Do you see a man skilled in his work? He will serve before kings; he will not serve before obscure men' (29); and then a paragraph about social etiquette, presumably taken from the pattern of behaviour in the royal court.

Chapter 23 opens with three verses concerned with social etiquette at high-class dinner parties: behave appropriately in the presence of your host (*note well who is before you*, 1, mg.); be very careful not to let your appetite run away with your manners (2), and beware of gluttony (2–3).

> *When you sit to dine with a ruler,*
> *note well what is before you,*
> *²and put a knife to your throat*
> *if you are given to gluttony.*
> *³Do not crave his delicacies,*
> *for that food is deceptive.*

The teacher now offers us a piece of financial advice and warns us again of the damaging effects of greed (23:4–8). Riches are so transient. One *glance*, and they can *fly* away *like an eagle* (or perhaps it means 'vulture'!). The section ends with a strange little admonition about not sitting down to eat with misers. Their attitude will only make you sick!

The next paragraph (23:9–13) covers some of the themes we have already noted: avoidance of the fool, not moving a neighbour's boundary stone, willingness to discipline a child. Of particular note, however, is the reference to God as the Defender of the fatherless.

> *Do not speak to a fool,*
> *for he will scorn the wisdom of your words.*
> *¹⁰Do not move an ancient boundary stone*
> *or encroach on the fields of the fatherless,*
> *¹¹for their Defender is strong;*
> *he will take up their case against you.*
> *¹²Apply your heart to instruction*
> *and your ears to words of knowledge.*
> *¹³Do not withhold discipline from a child;*
> *if you punish him with the rod, he will not die.*

As we noticed earlier (p. 114), the word 'Defender' (11) is *gō'ēl*, the kinsman-redeemer who takes up the case of those in need, especially to buy back property which the owner had been forced through poverty to sell. The *gō'ēl* (*cf.* Lv. 25:25; Dt. 19:12) features prominently in the story of Ruth (Ru. 2:26; 3:9; 4:1ff.), in which Boaz finds himself acting as kingsman-redeemer to safeguard the interests of Ruth and Naomi. It stresses the solidarity of the kinship group and the responsibility to act as redeemer (to buy back what rightfully belongs to one's blood relatives). But it also reflects an even deeper bond: that of covenant loyalty. In Ruth, the word is used of Boaz' covenant commitment to Ruth and Naomi to identify himself with them so that he could act on their behalf and for their good. As in Job 19:25, however, the word here in Proverbs 23:11 is applied directly to God. God is their kinsman-redeemer who will *take up* their *case*. God is bound in covenant loyalty to his people, especially the poor. This phrase *take up* their *case* is 'a forensic term, but is here used metaphorically of Yahweh's protection of the poor. When Yahweh "pleads someone's cause" the phrase is equivalent to his vindicating that person and executing judgement against his opponents.'[2]

The elderly and the powerful (23:15 – 24:22)

This section feels even more like a return to the style of Proverbs 1 – 9. We, the readers, are again addressed as 'My son', and several times it is suggested that the young man should *Listen to your father* (23:22), *Listen . . . and be wise* (23:19).

This fatherly talking again includes practical advice. Again we hear the words *be zealous for the fear of the LORD* (23:17); we are reminded of the temptations of getting in with the wrong crowd (23:20–21); and we are cautioned against the lure of the prostitute (23:27). There is also a very strong warning against the dangers of drunkenness (23:29–35). There is a tender paragraph in 23:22–25, of which Wolff writes: 'The wisdom of Proverbs shows . . . how concrete problems of the care of the old have to be solved through a person's behaviour to his parents.'[3]

> *Listen to your father, who gave you life,*
> *and do not despise your mother when she is old.*
> [23]*Buy the truth and do not sell it;*
> *get wisdom, discipline and understanding.*
> [24]*The father of a righteous man has great joy;*
> *he who has a wise son delights in him.*
> [25]*May your father and mother be glad;*
> *may she who gave you birth rejoice!*

When parents get old, children are no longer asked first of all whether they are obedient or disobedient; the question is whether they are considerate to their parents or despise them, whether they are a joy or a sorrow to them.[4]

At the centre of this section is another little vignette about Wisdom herself (24:3–4). Here the domestic side of Wisdom's concerns is uppermost. Building the house and filling its rooms with furniture are part of the celebration of family life which we have noticed before. To see a house well built and decorated with treasures is a sign to the author that there is blessing from God.

---

[2] Whybray, *Proverbs*, p. 329, quoting the RSV.
[3] H. W. Wolff, *Anthropology of the Old Testament* (SCM, 1974), p. 183.
[4] *Ibid.*

David Hubbard comments: 'In a society that was still learning what it meant to walk by faith, the tangible present rewards were a keen incentive to follow God's ways.'[5] There is also an unmistakable echo here of the house which Wisdom herself built, with its seven pillars, referred to in 9:1. There Wisdom was inviting us to come into the house to be fed with life-giving food, in contrast to the house of Folly, with its graveyard behind (9:18).

This vignette, however, is set in a context which speaks both of wicked people whose hearts plot violence (2), and of the importance of power and knowledge (5–6). It is saying, in other words, that Wisdom is important in public as well as in private life. Wisdom is the true power in society. It is not the wicked plotters who have the real power, but those who are wise and have knowledge.[6]

> *Do not envy wicked men,*
> *do not desire their company;*
> *²for their hearts plot violence,*
> *and their lips talk about making trouble.*
> *³By wisdom a house is built,*
> *and through understanding it is established;*
> *⁴through knowledge its rooms are filled*
> *with rare and beautiful treasures.*
> *⁵A wise man has great power,*
> *and a man of knowledge increases strength;*
> *⁶for waging war you need guidance,*
> *and for victory many advisers.*

Wisdom is therefore also relevant to situations of conflict (5–6), giving strength in battle. And Wisdom's voice must also be heard *at the gate* (7), the place of the administration of legal justice, and the home of government. In domestic and national life, therefore, in security and in conflict, Wisdom's voice is speaking and needs to be heard.

The specific teachings from the father to his son in these two chapters (23 and 24) do not add very much new material to that which we have already met. Wisdom and knowledge are greater than physical strength (24:5), and are as *honey* to the *soul*, giving sweet satisfaction and *a future hope* (24:13–14). A decision is called for: the son should *keep* his *heart on the right path* (23:19). *Truth, wisdom, discipline and understanding* are there for the effort of 'buying' them (23:23).

---

[5] Hubbard, p. 371.
[6] *Cf.* Wolff, *op. cit.*, p. 209.

Wisdom and justice in law and at work (24:23–34)

This group of 'further sayings of the wise' gives us some practical wisdom on straight speaking, impartiality, honesty (23–26), and the problems of being vengeful (28–29) and of laziness (30–34). Hubbard helpfully categorizes them under the headings of 'Partiality in Law' (24:23–26); 'Sound Priorities' (24:27); 'Honesty in Court' (24:28–29) and 'Industry in Work' (24:30–34). We have come across these themes before, though they do not feature much in the first set of sayings of the wise.

> *These also are sayings of the wise:*
>
> > *To show partiality in judging is not good:*
> > ²⁴*Whoever says to the guilty, 'You are innocent' –*
> > *peoples will curse him and nations denounce him.*
> > ²⁵*But it will go well with those who convict the guilty,*
> > *and rich blessing will come upon them.*
> >
> > ²⁶*An honest answer*
> > *is like a kiss on the lips.*
> >
> > ²⁷*Finish your outdoor work and get your fields ready;*
> > *after that, build your house.*
> >
> > ²⁸*Do not testify against your neighbour without cause,*
> > *or use your lips to deceive.*
> > ²⁹*Do not say, 'I'll do to him as he has done to me;*
> > *I'll pay that man back for what he did.'*
> >
> > ³⁰*I went past the field of the sluggard,*
> > *past the vineyard of the man who lacks judgment;*
> > ³¹*thorns had come up everywhere,*
> > *the ground was covered with weeds,*
> > *and the stone wall was in ruins.*
> > ³²*I applied my heart to what I observed*
> > *and learned a lesson from what I saw:*
> > ³³*A little sleep, a little slumber,*
> > *a little folding of the hands to rest –*
> > ³⁴*and poverty will come on you like a bandit*
> > *and scarcity like an armed man.*

We can pick out a few gems to concentrate on. *An honest answer is like a kiss on the lips* (26). Such a kiss is a mark of true friendshp; so is straightforward honest speech. On the other hand, if we show partiality in judging, that is not good.

The sound priorities of verse 27 probably refer to the setting up of a home before marriage. Toy suggests: 'First acquire the means of supporting a family, then thou mayest marry, and accomplish thy desire to build thee a house.'[7] Scott compares this verse with Jesus' teaching in Luke's gospel about counting the cost of buiilding a tower before starting construction (Lk. 14:28). It is wise for us to take stock, weigh possibilities and consider consequences before acting.

Verses 28 and 29 continue a theme we have noticed earlier, against taking revenge; and 30–34 parallel the paragraph in 6:6–11 with its teaching against laziness. Hubbard again has a pointed comment: 'The parallel between "lazy man" and "devoid of understanding" makes clear that the laziness in view was not the result of a weak back but a hollow brain. Not strength but will was the lack.'[8] Here it is encapsulated in a little moral story which gives an example of a lesson learned.

Proverbs of Solomon: Hezekiah's edition (25:1 – 29:27)

The next four chapters include a collection which is said to come from Solomon, or Solomon's training schools, brought together and edited by Hezekiah's scribes, who have tended to group the sayings together a little more than in the earlier collection from Solomon. We will not spend a great deal of time on this section, as we have met much of the material before. There are, however, several occasions in these chapters when Wisdom's imagination is working particularly effectively. A quick glance through chapter 25, for example, draws vivid pictures of *the heavens* (3), *the silversmith* (4) and the courtroom (8). The writers refer to *apples of gold in settings of silver* (11), ear-rings and ornaments (12). The weather, food, archery, clothing, agriculture and the city walls all serve as images for these proverbs. From this variety, let us pick out a few topics for further discussion. In a sense, however, the real value of these chapters is absorbed simply through reading the text itself, and allowing the author to jar our imagination into action, so as to let the proverb speak directly to us. Commentary and application can sometimes get too much in the way!

Chapter 25 opens (2–8) with details of life at *court* (*cf.* also 16:10–15). The responsibilities of the king are underlined, but very much also with an eye to the duties of the courtiers.

> *It is the glory of God to conceal a matter;*
> *to search out a matter is the glory of kings.*

---

[7] Toy, p. 453.
[8] Hubbard, p. 383, quoting the RSV.

³*As the heavens are high and the earth is deep,*
  so the hearts of kings are unsearchable.

⁴*Remove the dross from the silver,*
  and out comes material for the silversmith;
⁵*remove the wicked from the king's presence,*
  and his throne will be established through righteousness.

⁶*Do not exalt yourself in the king's presence,*
  and do not claim a place among great men;
⁷*it is better for him to say to you, 'Come up here,'*
  than for him to humiliate you before a nobleman.

What you have seen with your eyes
⁸ *do not bring hastily to court,*
for what will you do in the end
  if your neighbour puts you to shame?

We learn that it is part of the king's role to *search out* the detail of *a matter* so that wise judgments and decisions can be made, even though this takes place before the mystery of the ways of God (25:2). But just as the king cannot search the heart of God, so the king's subjects cannot search the king's heart (25:3). The king's throne must *be established through righteousness* (25:5), and he should expect a humble response from his courtiers (25:6).

From verse 11 of chapter 25, the style becomes distinctive. Many of the verses follow this pattern: 'Like an A is B.' By sketching very unexpected comparisons between certain A's and B's, the writer provokes us to think about some moral lesson or other. Many of the most surprising – and therefore most memorable – proverbs come in these chapters.

A word aptly spoken
  is like apples of gold in settings of silver.

¹²*Like an ear-ring of gold or an ornament of fine gold*
  is a wise man's rebuke to a listening ear.

¹³*Like the coolness of snow at harvest time*
  is a trustworthy messenger to those who send him;
  he refreshes the spirit of his masters.

¹⁴*Like clouds and wind without rain*
  is a man who boasts of gifts he does not give.

¹⁵*Through patience a ruler can be persuaded,*
  and a gentle tongue can break a bone.

[16] *If you find honey, eat just enough –*
   too much of it, and you will vomit.

[17] *Seldom set foot in your neighbour's house –*
   too much of you, and he will hate you.

[18] *Like a club or a sword or a sharp arrow*
   is the man who gives false testimony against his neighbour.

[19] *Like a bad tooth or a lame foot*
   is reliance on the unfaithful in times of trouble.

[20] *Like one who takes away a garment on a cold day,*
   or like vinegar poured on soda,
   is one who sings songs to a heavy heart.

[21] *If your enemy is hungry, give him food to eat;*
   if he is thirsty, give him water to drink.
[22] *In doing this, you will heap burning coals on his head,*
   and the LORD will reward you.

[23] *As a north wind brings rain,*
   so a sly tongue brings angry looks.

[24] *Better to live on a corner of the roof*
   than share a house with a quarrelsome wife.

In this chapter there are a number of references to appropriate speech, among them the lovely picture of verse 11: *A word aptly spoken is like apples of gold in settings of silver*; and verse 13: *Like the coolness of snow at harvest time is a trustworthy messenger to those who send him; he refreshes the spirit of his masters.* By contrast, inappropriate and boastful speech is as unhelpful as *clouds and wind without rain* (14).

The chapter includes some famous comments (repeated elsewhere in Proverbs) on the importance of generosity. This is a theme picked up in the New Testament (Rom. 12:19–20): *If your enemy is hungry, give him food to eat; if he is thirsty, give him water to drink. In doing this, you will heap burning coals on his head, and the LORD will reward you* (21–22). The reference to *burning coals* may possibly refer to divine punishment, and indicate that to do your enemy good will only make his punishment worse if he does not repent. Much more likely, it signifies 'the burning pangs of shame and contrition'.[9]

It also has this vivid social comment: *Better to live on a corner of the roof than share a house with a quarrelsome wife* (24).

---

[9] *Cf.* C. E. B. Cranfield, *Romans: A Shorter Commentary* (T. and T. Clark, 1985) on Rom. 12:19–20.

The pictorial imagery of the last four verses of chapter 25 is used to good effect to illustrate the themes of relief on hearing *good news* (25), the dangers of compromise (26), the dangers of excess (27), and the importance of *self-control* (28).

> Like cold water to a weary soul
>   is good news from a distant land.
> ²⁶Like a muddied spring or a polluted well
>   is a righteous man who gives way to the wicked.
> ²⁷It is not good to eat too much honey,
>   nor is it honourable to seek one's own honour.
> ²⁸Like a city whose walls are broken down
>   is a man who lacks self-control.

Chapter 26 includes a long exposé of the folly of fools (1–12) and the laziness of sluggards (13–16).

The first part (1–12) all focuses again on the fool. Toy describes these verses as a 'string of sarcasm'. To *honour* a fool is as inappropriate as *snow in summer or rain in harvest* time (1). An *undeserved curse*, such as a fool might give, is as aimless as a *fluttering* bird (2). A fool is not controlled by appeal to reason (3). Don't descend to the fool's level yourself (4–5). It is as useless to send *a message* by a fool as it is dangerous to cut off your own legs (6). The fool's attempts to cope with the sayings of wisdom are as futile as *a lame man* trying to jump (7).

Verses 13–16 pick up again the problem of the sluggard, who is scornfully attacked as stupid – for staying in bed on the pretext that there is *a lion* loose in the street (13–14) – though unaware of his stupidity (15–16).

What is of particular interest for us in chapter 26 is the way in which the author draws on the world of nature for his comparisons: the *snow* (1), the *rain* (1), the *fluttering sparrow* (2), the *darting swallow* (2), the *horse* (3), the *donkey* (3), the *thornbush* (9), the *dog* (11), the *lion* (13) – all are used to make the point in vivid word pictures. It is as if to underline Wisdom's concern for the whole of creation. The rest of the created order has things to teach us stupid and lazy humans about life!

> Like snow in summer or rain in harvest,
>   honour is not fitting for a fool.
>
> ²Like a fluttering sparrow or a darting swallow,
>   an undeserved curse does not come to rest.
>
> ³A whip for the horse, a halter for the donkey,
>   and a rod for the backs of fools!

*⁴Do not answer a fool according to his folly,
or you will be like him yourself.*

*⁵Answer a fool according to his folly,
or he will be wise in his own eyes.*

*⁶Like cutting off one's feet or drinking violence
is the sending of a message by the hand of a fool.*

*⁷Like a lame man's legs that hang limp
is a proverb in the mouth of a fool.*

*⁸Like tying a stone in a sling
is the giving of honour to a fool.*

*⁹Like a thornbush in a drunkard's hand
is a proverb in the mouth of a fool.*

*¹⁰Like an archer who wounds at random
is he who hires a fool or any passer-by.*

*¹¹As a dog returns to its vomit,
so a fool repeats his folly.*

*¹²Do you see a man wise in his own eyes?
There is more hope for a fool than for him.*

*¹³The sluggard says, 'There is a lion in the road,
a fierce lion roaming the streets!'*

*¹⁴As a door turns on its hinges,
so a sluggard turns on his bed.*

*¹⁵The sluggard buries his hand in the dish;
he is too lazy to bring it back to his mouth.*

*¹⁶The sluggard is wiser in his own eyes
than seven men who answer discreetly.*

Then follows a collection, including some extreme language (26:22–28), which teaches that gossip, malicious speech, deception and lying speech from an evil heart can all be exceedingly hurtful and damaging.

There are comments in chapter 27 about boasting (1–2), jealousy (3–4) and the value of a friend's rebuke (6). Verse 8 reminds us that there is no place like home: *Like a bird that strays from its nest is a man who strays from his home.* There are comments on prudence and hypocrisy (11–14), and domestic strife (15). Faithfulness, greed, and folly are all explored (17–22), and the chapter ends with an agricultural scene on the treatment of animals (23–27).

Do not boast about tomorrow,
  for you do not know what a day may bring forth.

²*Let another praise you, and not your own mouth;*
  someone else, and not your own lips.

³*Stone is heavy and sand a burden,*
  but provocation by a fool is heavier than both.

⁴*Anger is cruel and fury overwhelming,*
  but who can stand before jealousy?

⁵*Better is open rebuke*
  than hidden love.

⁶*Wounds from a friend can be trusted,*
  but an enemy multiplies kisses.

⁷*He who is full loathes honey,*
  but to the hungry even what is bitter tastes sweet.

⁸*Like a bird that strays from its nest*
  is a man who strays from his home.

⁹*Perfume and incense bring joy to the heart,*
  and the pleasantness of one's friend springs from his earnest counsel.

¹⁰*Do not forsake your friend and the friend of your father,*
  and do not go to your brother's house when disaster strikes you –
  better a neighbour nearby than a brother far away.

¹¹*Be wise, my son, and bring joy to my heart;*
  then I can answer anyone who treats me with contempt.

¹²*The prudent see danger and take refuge,*
  but the simple keep going and suffer for it.

¹³*Take the garment of one who puts up security for a stranger;*
  hold it in pledge if he does it for a wayward woman.

¹⁴*If a man loudly blesses his neighbour early in the morning,*
  it will be taken as a curse.

¹⁵*A quarrelsome wife is like*
  a constant dripping on a rainy day;
¹⁶*restraining her is like restraining the wind*
  or grasping oil with the hand.

¹⁷*As iron sharpens iron,*
  so one man sharpens another.

¹⁸*He who tends a fig-tree will eat its fruit,*
  and he who looks after his master will be honoured.

¹⁹As water reflects a face,
so a man's heart reflects the man.

²⁰Death and Destruction are never satisfied,
and neither are the eyes of man.

²¹The crucible for silver and the furnace for gold,
but man is tested by the praise he receives.

²²Though you grind a fool in a mortar,
grinding him like grain with a pestle,
you will not remove his folly from him.

²³Be sure you know the condition of your flocks,
give careful attention to your herds;
²⁴for riches do not endure for ever,
and a crown is not secure for all generations.
²⁵When the hay is removed and new growth appears
and the grass from the hills is gathered in,
²⁶the lambs will provide you with clothing,
and the goats with the price of a field.
²⁷You will have plenty of goats' milk
to feed you and your family
and to nourish your servant girls.

In these verses we find a range of work situations: the servant (18) *who tends the fig tree*; the shepherd (23–27) who needs to give careful attention to the *flocks*; the farmer (25; *cf.* 28:19) who works on the land. These all illustrate for us the importance of industry, the place of work in God's ordering of things, and our place as stewards of God's created order.

Perhaps this section is included here in chapter 27 because most of the young men in the training schools might well have come from landowning families. It is a salutary reminder that aspiring to national leadership does not mean letting go of the basic necessities by which families are fed and *servant girls* are nourished.

Chapter 27 also talks about love – which, we discover, should not be too cautious about saying what needs to be said (5), but should be expressed in loyal friendship (10).

Chapter 28 includes some thoughts on social justice, partly in relation to the duties of the rulers, but also more generally reinforcing the concern for *the poor* which we have already seen several times.

Note in particular the link in chapter 28 between justice and spiritual life: *Evil men do not understand justice, but those who seek the Lord understand it fully* (5); *If anyone turns a deaf ear to the law, even his prayers are detestable* (9); *He who gives to the poor will lack nothing, but he who closes his eyes to them receives many curses* (27):

> *The wicked man flees though no-one pursues,*
>   *but the righteous are as bold as a lion.*

> [2]*When a country is rebellious, it has many rulers,*
>   *but a man of understanding and knowledge maintains order.*

> [3]*A ruler who oppresses the poor*
>   *is like a driving rain that leaves no crops.*

> [4]*Those who forsake the law praise the wicked,*
>   *but those who keep the law resist them.*

> [5]*Evil men do not understand justice,*
>   *but those who seek the* LORD *understand it fully.*

> [6]*Better a poor man whose walk is blameless*
>   *than a rich man whose ways are perverse.*

> [7]*He who keeps the law is a discerning son,*
>   *but a companion of gluttons disgraces his father.*

> [8]*He who increases his wealth by exorbitant interest*
>   *amasses it for another, who will be kind to the poor.*

> [9]*If anyone turns a deaf ear to the law,*
>   *even his prayers are detestable.*

> [10]*He who leads the upright along an evil path*
>   *will fall into his own trap,*
>   *but the blameless will receive a good inheritance.*

> [11]*A rich man may be wise in his own eyes,*
>   *but a poor man who has discernment sees through him.*

> [12]*When the righteous triumph, there is great elation;*
>   *but when the wicked rise to power, men go into hiding.*

> [13]*He who conceals his sins does not prosper,*
>   *but whoever confesses and renounces them finds mercy.*

> [14]*Blessed is the man who always fears the* LORD,
>   *but he who hardens his heart falls into trouble.*

> [15]*Like a roaring lion or a charging bear*
>   *is a wicked man ruling over a helpless people.*

> [16]*A tyrannical ruler lacks judgment,*
>   *but he who hates ill-gotten gain will enjoy a long life.*

¹⁷A man tormented by the guilt of murder
  will be a fugitive till death;
  let no-one support him.

¹⁸He whose walk is blameless is kept safe,
  but he whose ways are perverse will suddenly fall.

¹⁹He who works his land will have abundant food,
  but the one who chases fantasies will have his fill of poverty.

²⁰A faithful man will be richly blessed,
  but one eager to get rich will not go unpunished.

²¹To show partiality is not good –
  yet a man will do wrong for a piece of bread.

²²A stingy man is eager to get rich
  and is unaware that poverty awaits him.

²³He who rebukes a man will in the end gain more favour
  than he who has a flattering tongue.

²⁴He who robs his father or mother
  and says, 'It's not wrong' –
  he is partner to him who destroys.

²⁵A greedy man stirs up dissension,
  but he who trusts in the LORD will prosper.

²⁶He who trusts in himself is a fool,
  but he who walks in wisdom is kept safe.

²⁷He who gives to the poor will lack nothing,
  but he who closes his eyes to them receives many curses.

²⁸When the wicked rise to power, people go into hiding;
  but when the wicked perish, the righteous thrive.

The chapter again contrasts *the righteous* and godly man with *the
wicked*. We find the importance of the confession of sin stressed in
verse 13: *He who conceals his sins does not prosper, but whoever
confesses and renounces them finds mercy.*

Justice is again one of the themes of chapter 29. There is an apt
comment on sleaze in government: *By justice a king gives a country
stability, but one who is greedy for bribes tears it down* (4); *The
righteous care about justice for the poor, but the wicked have no such
concern* (7). None the less, ultimately justice is from the LORD:
*Many seek an audience with a ruler, but it is from the LORD that
man gets justice* (26).

Chapter 29 has wise sayings with provocative points to make us think about family loyalty (3), the snare of sin (6), the dangers of mockery (8), the value of self-control (11), the importance of taking care with our words (20), and the damage done by hot temper and pride (22–23):

> *A man who remains stiff-necked after many rebukes*
> *will suddenly be destroyed – without remedy.*
>
> ²*When the righteous thrive, the people rejoice;*
> *when the wicked rule, the people groan.*
>
> ³*A man who loves wisdom brings joy to his father,*
> *but a companion of prostitutes squanders his wealth.*
>
> ⁴*By justice a king gives a country stability,*
> *but one who is greedy for bribes tears it down.*
>
> ⁵*Whoever flatters his neighbour*
> *is spreading a net for his feet.*
>
> ⁶*An evil man is snared by his own sin,*
> *but a righteous one can sing and be glad.*
>
> ⁷*The righteous care about justice for the poor,*
> *but the wicked have no such concern.*
>
> ⁸*Mockers stir up a city,*
> *but wise men turn away anger.*
>
> ⁹*If a wise man goes to court with a fool,*
> *the fool rages and scoffs, and there is no peace.*
>
> ¹⁰*Bloodthirsty men hate a man of integrity*
> *and seek to kill the upright.*
>
> ¹¹*A fool gives full vent to his anger,*
> *but a wise man keeps himself under control.*
>
> ¹²*If a ruler listens to lies,*
> *all his officials become wicked.*
>
> ¹³*The poor man and the oppressor have this in common:*
> *The LORD gives sight to the eyes of both.*
>
> ¹⁴*If a king judges the poor with fairness,*
> *his throne will always be secure.*
>
> ¹⁵*The rod of correction imparts wisdom,*
> *but a child left to himself disgraces his mother.*
>
> ¹⁶*When the wicked thrive, so does sin,*
> *but the righteous will see their downfall.*

¹⁷Discipline your son, and he will give you peace;
he will bring delight to your soul.

¹⁸Where there is no revelation, the people cast off restraint;
but blessed is he who keeps the law.

¹⁹A servant cannot be corrected by mere words;
though he understands, he will not respond.

²⁰Do you see a man who speaks in haste?
There is more hope for a fool than for him.

²¹If a man pampers his servant from youth,
he will bring grief in the end.

²²An angry man stirs up dissension,
and a hot-tempered one commits many sins.

²³A man's pride brings him low,
but a man of lowly spirit gains honour.

²⁴The accomplice of a thief is his own enemy;
he is put under oath and dare not testify.

²⁵Fear of man will prove to be a snare,
but whoever trusts in the LORD is kept safe.

²⁶Many seek an audience with a ruler,
but it is from the LORD that man gets justice.

²⁷The righteous detest the dishonest;
the wicked detest the upright.

Sayings of Agur (30:1–33)

Chapter 30 offers us what some versions translate as *an oracle*, which usually means the message of one of God's prophets, or the chant of a seer. Alternatively, the word may refer to the place from which Agur comes (see NIV text and margin).

The sayings of Agur son of Jakeh – an oracle:

This man declared to Ithiel,
to Ithiel and to Ucal:

²'I am the most ignorant of men;
I do not have a man's understanding.
³I have not learned wisdom,
nor have I knowledge of the Holy One.
⁴Who has gone up to heaven and come down?
Who has gathered up the wind in the hollow of his hands?

161

> *Who has wrapped up the waters in his cloak?*
>   *Who has established all the ends of the earth?*
> *What is his name, and the name of his son?*
>   *Tell me if you know!*
>
> ⁵*"Every word of God is flawless;*
>   *he is a shield to those who take refuge in him.*
> ⁶*Do not add to his words,*
>   *or he will rebuke you and prove you a liar.'*

It may be that Ithiel and Ucal (2) are the names of people, but, with a different word division of the Hebrew text, these words could be translated something like: 'I am weary, O God! I am weary and faint!' (see NIV mg.). The Anchor Bible even offers: 'There is no God! There is no God and I cannot know anything!' The suggestion which follows from taking this second view is that this section is a dialogue between Agur, regarded as a sceptic (1–4), and an orthodox believer (5–6). Verses 7–9 would then be a prayer to Yahweh that the believer may never be tempted to such a denial of God. There is no reason, however, why Agur, Ithiel and Ucal should not all be people about whom we know virtually nothing at all.

One of the things which *are* clear is that this oracle, associated with Agur, son of Jakeh, uses the world of nature as an object lesson for moral guidance. The rationality inherent in the natural order is from the same Creator as are we human beings. It is no wonder that there is some correspondence between it and us. Our human trouble is that we are too proud, exalting ourselves, whereas (on one reading of this section), from his own example (2–3) and from his teaching (4–6), Agur urges a proper humility. At least, that is what he seems to be doing. Others take the declaration to be rather heavily sarcastic: 'There are people around who claim to know God perfectly; I am not in that class!' Verse 4 is paralleled in the later chapters of the book of Job, but ends with the ironic comment, 'Tell me if you know!' There is, however, one clear way in which we can approach these compellingly mysterious verses. Agur is a humble man trying to make sense of his world, and frustrated by the claims to wisdom from others. Maybe he stands for those who know that they do not know very much about God and his ways. It is really not very clear who is saying what in this paragraph, but its conclusion is unmistakable: *Every word of God is flawless; he is a shield to those who take refuge in him* (5). The route to knowledge begins with God (5–6).

What is needed is a recognition of the revelation of God. God makes himself known. God speaks his word. What is needed is the honesty to accept this and a willingness to learn from the world he has made (18–19). It is the way of Wisdom alone which brings a person to receive God's revelatory word. It is Wisdom which brings knowledge of *the Holy One* (3).

> ⁷*'Two things I ask of you, O LORD;*
> *do not refuse me before I die:*
> ⁸*Keep falsehood and lies far from me;*
> *give me neither poverty nor riches,*
> *but give me only my daily bread.*
> ⁹*Otherwise, I may have too much and disown you*
> *and say, "Who is the LORD?"*
> *Or I may become poor and steal,*
> *and so dishonour the name of my God.'*

This little section fits in with the view that Agur is a humble man. He prays for God to help him, because he knows his own weaknesses in the face of riches. It is too easy to forget that everything we have comes from God. We need help to use both poverty and wealth appropriately.

> ¹⁰*'Do not slander a servant to his master,*
> *or he will curse you, and you will pay for it.*
>
> ¹¹*'There are those who curse their fathers*
> *and do not bless their mothers;*
> ¹²*those who are pure in their own eyes*
> *and yet are not cleansed of their filth;*
> ¹³*those whose eyes are ever so haughty,*
> *whose glances are so disdainful;*
> ¹⁴*those whose teeth are swords*
> *and whose jaws are set with knives*
> *to devour the poor from the earth,*
> *the needy from among mankind.*
>
> ¹⁵*'The leech has two daughters.*
> *"Give! Give!" they cry.*
>
> *'There are three things that are never satisfied,*
> *four that never say, "Enough!":*
> ¹⁶*the grave, the barren womb,*
> *land, which is never satisfied with water,*
> *and fire, which never says, "Enough!"*
>
> ¹⁷*'The eye that mocks a father,*
> *that scorns obedience to a mother,*
> *will be pecked out by the ravens of the valley,*
> *will be eaten by the vultures.*

¹⁸'*There are three things that are too amazing for me,*
    four that I do not understand:
¹⁹*the way of an eagle in the sky,*
    the way of a snake on a rock,
the way of a ship on the high seas,
    and the way of a man with a maiden.

²⁰'*This is the way of an adulteress:*
    She eats and wipes her mouth
    and says, "I've done nothing wrong."

²¹'*Under three things the earth trembles,*
    under four it cannot bear up:
²²*a servant who becomes king,*
    a fool who is full of food,
²³*an unloved woman who is married,*
    and a maidservant who displaces her mistress.

²⁴'*Four things on earth are small,*
    yet they are extremely wise:
²⁵*Ants are creatures of little strength,*
    yet they store up their food in the summer;
²⁶*conies are creatures of little power,*
    yet they make their home in the crags;
²⁷*locusts have no king,*
    yet they advance together in ranks;
²⁸*A lizard can be caught with the hand,*
    yet it is found in kings' palaces.

²⁹'*There are three things that are stately in their stride,*
    four that move with stately bearing:
³⁰*a lion, mighty among beasts,*
    who retreats before nothing;
³¹*a strutting cock, a he-goat,*
    and a king with his army around him.

³²'*If you have played the fool and exalted yourself,*
    or if you have planned evil,
    clap your hand over your mouth!
³³*For as churning the milk produces butter,*
    and as twisting the nose produces blood,
    so stirring up anger produces strife.'

The chapter concludes with a collection of rather unconnected thoughts about telling tales (10), four sorts of sinners (11–14), a *leech* (15a), four things that will not be satisfied (15b–16), a scornful son (17), four amazing things (18–19), the *adulteress* (20), four people it is hard to cope with (21–23), four *small* creatures (24–28), four proud creatures (29–31), and a brief couple of verses at the end about folly.

There are, in this list, several sets of 'counting' proverbs, in which numbers of things are added up. Usually the style is: 'There are three things . . . four . . .' We met this style before in 6:16 ('There are six things the LORD hates, seven that are detestable to him'). It is a device used in other examples of Semitic poetry, perhaps for the sake of emphasis, or to aid learning. Perhaps these numerical proverbs also reflect something about the ordering of the world and the God who orders it.

Thoughts from the queen mother (31:1–9)

The sayings of King Lemuel – an oracle his mother taught him:

> ²'*O my son, O son of my womb,*
> *O son of my vows,*
> ³*do not spend your strength on women,*
> *your vigour on those who ruin kings.*
>
> ⁴'*It is not for kings, O Lemuel –*
> *not for kings to drink wine,*
> *not for rulers to crave beer,*
> ⁵*lest they drink and forget what the law decrees,*
> *and deprive all the oppressed of their rights.*
> ⁶*Give beer to those who are perishing,*
> *wine to those who are in anguish;*
> ⁷*let them drink and forget their poverty*
> *and remember their misery no more.*
>
> ⁸'*Speak up for those who cannot speak for themselves,*
> *for the rights of all who are destitute.*
> ⁹*Speak up and judge fairly;*
> *defend the rights of the poor and needy.*'

This little oracle was taught to King Lemuel by his mother. (The words *King Lemuel – an oracle* could be translated as 'Lemuel, king of Massa' (see NIV mg.), a territory in North Arabia.)[10] The queen mother could have had some considerable say at court (*cf.* 1 Ki. 15:13; 2 Ki. 11:1). This paragraph sums up what is needed in a good ruler. Picking up some of the themes we have noticed before, Lemuel's mother is concerned first about the dangers of loose

---

[10] *Cf.* Whybray, *Proverbs*, p. 422.

women and the misuse of alcohol. But her reason is that their influence may prevent the king from remembering why he is king: to care for *the poor* and suffering, to *speak up for those who cannot speak up for themselves*, to stand up *for the rights of the destitute*, and to *defend the rights of the poor and needy*. A major duty of the king is provision for the well-being of his people, and especially to safeguard the rights of the helpless. Here is a kingliness of service, a kingdom of benevolence, a kingly rule in which people come first.

Epilogue: The wife of noble character: Wisdom at home (31:10–31)

The book of Proverbs concludes by describing in a vivid acrostic poem the virtues of an excellent wife. Each verse begins with a different letter of the Hebrew alphabet, using the twenty-two letters in sequence. This formal arrangement means that there is not necessarily a logical connection between one verse and the next. The acrostic form may have been used not only to highlight the beautiful order of its subject matter, and as an expression of wholeness (*i.e.* 'from A to Z'), but also probably as a learning device to help the reader remember it.

> *A wife of noble character who can find?*
> *She is worth far more than rubies.*
> [11] *Her husband has full confidence in her*
> *and lacks nothing of value.*
> [12] *She brings him good, not harm,*
> *all the days of her life.*
> [13] *She selects wool and flax*
> *and works with eager hands.*
> [14] *She is like the merchant ships,*
> *bringing her food from afar.*
> [15] *She gets up while it is still dark;*
> *she provides food for her family*
> *and portions for her servant girls.*
> [16] *She considers a field and buys it;*
> *out of her earnings she plants a vineyard.*
> [17] *She sets about her work vigorously;*
> *her arms are strong for her tasks.*
> [18] *She sees that her trading is profitable,*
> *and her lamp does not go out at night.*
> [19] *In her hand she holds the distaff*
> *and grasps the spindle with her fingers.*
> [20] *She opens her arms to the poor*
> *and extends her hands to the needy.*
> [21] *When it snows, she has no fear for her household;*

for all of them are clothed in scarlet.
[22]*She makes coverings for her bed;*
 she is clothed in fine linen and purple.
[23]*Her husband is respected at the city gate,*
 where he takes his seat among the elders of the land.
[24]*She makes linen garments and sells them,*
 and supplies the merchants with sashes.
[25]*She is clothed with strength and dignity;*
 she can laugh at the days to come.
[26]*She speaks with wisdom,*
 and faithful instruction is on her tongue.
[27]*She watches over the affairs of her household*
 and does not eat the bread of idleness.
[28]*Her children arise and call her blessed;*
 her husband also, and he praises her:
[29]'*Many women do noble things,*
 but you surpass them all.'
[30]*Charm is deceptive, and beauty is fleeting;*
 but a woman who fears the LORD *is to be praised.*
[31]*Give her the reward she has earned,*
 and let her works bring her praise at the city gate.

The description is of a fairly ordinary home, based on what today we tend to call middle-class values. Whybray describes the setting of the poem: 'The picture – whether allegorical in intention or not – presented here is of a well-to-do family, neither aristocratic nor royal, which has achieved the prosperity and stability to which the peasant farmer of 10:1 – 22:16 aspired, and which is promised as a reward for decent, honest work in such proverbs as 28:19, 20.'[11] In other words, this picture answers to some of the aspirations of ordinary, hard-working people whose characteristics have been traced in earlier parts of the book. It is also of particular interest, given the high concentration of attention paid to men throughout Proverbs – the farmer, the son, the shepherd, the ruler, and so on – that the editor chooses to bring this collection to its climax by exalting the virtues of a woman. The woman here is not, as elsewhere, defined only in terms of the men in her life. That is important for us to note for a Christian community which is only slowly recognizing the alienating emphasis of the traditionally perceived 'maleness' of God (who is in reality beyond gender), of male dominance in the church's ministry, and of male language in Christian liturgies. This woman is very much her own person. She has extensive management responsibilities of her own.

---

[11] *Cf. ibid.*, p. 426.

Is this a marriage preparation book for young ladies? Or a courtship guide to help young men select a partner? We do not know. Is this, rather, a wonderful picture of what the life of Wisdom would look like, were Wisdom to be incarnate in an ordinary home? There is an idealism about these verses which, if we were to take them today as a description of wifely virtues, would make many Christian wives feel that they do not match up, and would certainly make many Christian husbands run away scared. Let us see what would happen if we understood these paragraphs as a description of ·Wisdom at home.

The home includes work with *wool and flax* (13), and there are *servant girls* (15). There is money to buy a *field* and a *vineyard* (16), trade to be managed (18) and charity to be offered to the *poor* (20). There is enough fabric to make the house comfortable and warm (22), as well as to make *sashes* for the *merchants* (24). At its centre is *a wife of noble character* (1).

She is loving and faithful (12), careful and hard-working (13–15), prudent (16), *strong* (17) and diligent (18). She is generous (20), prepared (21), extravagant in care (22), dignified and good-humoured (25). She is wise (26) and watchful (27), and *fears the* LORD (30). No wonder her children bless her and her husband extols her (28–29) and the key people in the neighbourhood speak *her praise* (31)!

Such a person is rare indeed (10). This list would make most of us feel somewhat lacking. Indeed, if this passage were understood only in terms of a blueprint for a Christian wife (as some Christian books have been known to suggest!), it would be likely to induce such feelings of inadequacy that a woman could well come to believe that she was very far from what Winnicott calls 'good enough'.[12]

But there are strong hints here that we do need to see beyond this very ideal picture to something, or Someone, else. *She is worth far more than rubies*, we are told (10). We first read that of Wisdom in 3:15. She looks after the house, and *provides food* (13–15). We first read that of Wisdom in 9:1–6. She is a person of integrity and intelligence, speaking *with wisdom* and offering *faithful instruction* (26). We first read that of Wisdom in 4:5–6. So most likely what we have in this beautiful poem is not only the idealized picture of the wife whose noble character fills out the blessed life to which 'the fear of the LORD' leads. What we also have is a demonstration of what the life of Wisdom herself would look like, were she to manage the home. Wisdom is no esoteric concept which floats in some mystical

---

[12] D. W. Winnicott, child psychoanalyst, coined the phrase 'good enough mothering', which has become widely used. *Cf.* his *The Maturational Processes and the Facilitating Environment* (Hogarth, 1965).

realm, out of touch with the ordinary world. The Wisdom of God is here expressed in the creativity, responsibility and artistry of managing a home, providing for the needs of others, and taking a stand on the side of the poor.

When Wisdom is at home, *she brings . . . good* (12), takes trouble over her work (13–14), is diligent and hard-working (15–19), prudent and generous (20), loving and creative (21–24), strong and dignified (25) and concerned for the welfare, education and growth of others (26–27). Wisdom is praised in the privacy of the heart (29) and in the public place (31). Her rich and noble character is summed up in the statement that she *fears the LORD* (30). What a wonderful illustration we have here of Wisdom embodied, Wisdom lived out, Wisdom at home!

Conclusion
Godliness in working clothes[1]

We have sought to understand the message of Proverbs in terms of the character, methods, imagination, values and examples of Wisdom. We have described her as a personification of a particular aspect of the nature of God. It is God's delight that Wisdom evokes, God's creativity that Wisdom expresses, God's processes in history that Wisdom governs, and God's purposes for human life in this world that Wisdom teaches. Wisdom is that part of God's nature which creates, orders, sheds light and gives life. And especially in the early chapters of Proverbs, this aspect of God's nature is depicted as a woman, mysterious but powerful, speaking in the public realm but whose meanings are sometimes hidden, exploring, ordering, enthusing, celebrating, life-giving and life-enhancing.

Those who find Wisdom themselves begin to share her wise ways. Those who find Wisdom find God, life, meaning, and a way of managing in the messy complexities of day-to-day life in the world. They find a way of coping with life's stresses and uncertainties and discover something of the art of living. To live wisely, then, is to live in God's ways. To live in God's ways is to discover what being human is meant to be about.

The interesting thing about Proverbs is how unreligious the book is. There is nothing about the temple, the priests or sacrifice. There is a lot about street corners, houses, rooftops, jewels and animals. There is hardly anything about religious ceremonies. There is a lot about love, justice and concern for the poor. As Derek Kidner put it in a fine paragraph:

> It is a book which seldom takes you to church. Like its own figure of Wisdom, it calls across to you in the street about some everyday matter, or points things out at home. Its function in Scripture is to put godliness into working clothes; to name business and society

---

[1] A wonderful title which I have borrowed from Kidner, *Proverbs*, p. 35.

as spheres in which we are to acquit ourselves with credit to our Lord, and in which we are to look for His training.[2]

We have tried to explore some of those 'working clothes' in family life and marriage, in questions of health, security, food and, to some degree, the political realm. The 'conversation' in which we have to engage when our faith comes up against questions of living for God in the ordinary and the everyday is the way we learn, and the way our characters are helped to develop. There are many situations in which there are no answers. Proverbs does not very often deal in generalities. The writers, with wonderful pictures more often than not, describe a situation at home or at work, and draw some moral conclusion from it. They then put the questions to us: 'Is this like your situation? Are these your values? What does holding values like that mean in terms of how you should live now?' Proverbs, then, is not an easy book. To read it carefully will not only educate, inform, amuse and annoy, but it should change us as well. Constantly we are faced with choices which form part of the stories our lives are telling. Proverbs constantly reminds us that some choices are the way of Folly, and diminish, weaken and destabilize individual lives and communities. Others are the way of Wisdom.

Wisdom, then, becomes very practical. But, as Job 28:12 puts it, 'Where can wisdom be found?'

Most writers think that the personification of Wisdom in the Hebrew Bible is really a literary device. It speaks of this aspect of God's nature by speaking of Wisdom as a woman. It is pressing the Old Testament thought too far to suggest that here is some divine being separate from God. When we turn to some of the later wisdom literature in the Apocrypha, however, it does seem as though the writers had in mind much more of a divine figure (*Ecclesiasticus* 24:1ff., for example, and *Wisdom of . Solomon* 8:2–16, in which Solomon desires Wisdom to be his spouse). The language and imagery about Wisdom are by no means all straightforward. By the time we reach St Paul in the New Testament, there is still some ambiguity in the way the apostle speaks of wisdom. Sometimes wisdom is a characteristic in different ways both of God and of human beings, in the latter case referring to contemporary philosophies. Thus in 1 Corinthians 1:17 St Paul says that Christ sent him to preach the gospel not with words of human wisdom, lest the cross of Christ be emptied of its power. Then in verses 20–21 he contrasts divine and human wisdom:

Where is the wise man? Where is the scholar? Where is the

[2] *Ibid.*

philosopher of this age? Has not God made foolish the wisdom of the world? For since in the wisdom of God the world through its wisdom did not know him, God was pleased through the foolishness of what was preached to save those who believe.

In fact, in verse 19 Paul quotes Isaiah 29:14, 'I will destroy the wisdom of the wise' (which in Isaiah probably refers to foolish politicians), to contrast divine wisdom and the folly of the worldly-wise.

But then it becomes clear that Paul believes that God's Wisdom is not only wiser than human wisdom, but that it is something wonderfully separate altogether. A qualitative, not only a quantitative, distinction is being made. Paul seems here to be aligning himself with the wisdom tradition in the Hebrew Scriptures. There is a Wisdom which is different even from the very best of the worldly-wise. There is a wisdom from God – a Wisdom of God – which human beings of themselves cannot know. It is a Wisdom that can be received only through the gift of God himself:

We speak of God's secret wisdom, a wisdom that has been hidden and that God destined for our glory before time began. None of the rulers of this age understood it, for if they had, they would not have crucified the Lord of glory. However, as it is written:

No eye has seen,
    no ear has heard,
    no mind has conceived
        what God has prepared for those who love him –

but God has revealed it to us by his Spirit (1 Cor. 2:7–10).

Paul is moving to a deeper understanding of Wisdom even than Proverbs illustrates.[3] This deeper meaning seems to be forced on him because of his encounter with Jesus Christ 'who has become for us widsom from God' (1 Cor. 1:30). So where shall Wisdom be found? St Paul would answer: in Jesus Christ our Lord. He is God's Wisdom. He is God's delight. Through him God made the world. In him God's light shines. He embodies the life of God himself. As Paul argued elsewhere: 'See to it that no-one takes you captive through hollow and deceptive philosophy, which depends on human tradition and the basic principles of this world rather than on Christ. For in Christ all the fulness of the Deity lives in bodily form' (Col. 2:8–9).

He shares the life of God, creator, redeemer and giver of life. This

[3] *Cf.* the discussion in James Wood, *Wisdom Literature* (Duckworth, 1979), ch. 9.

is the basis for Paul's argument, in place after place, that it is through coming to reverent obedience to God ('the fear of the Lord') through Jesus Christ in the power of the Spirit, that we not only discover, but are also given strength to live out, godliness in working clothes. For what God in his Wisdom requires of us, that in Christ through his Spirit he also gives.

> Be thou my Wisdom, thou my true Word;
> I ever with thee, thou with me, Lord;
> Thou my great Father, I thy true son;
> Thou in me dwelling, and I with thee one.[4]

Amen.

---

[4] E. H. Hull and M. E. Byrne, 'Be thou my Vision' (from the ancient Irish).

Other titles in The Bible Speaks Today series

New Testament

The Bible Speaks Today: Bible Themes series